The Ideal King

The Ideal King

Jesus in Light of the Mosaic Ideal

JOHN K. GRANT

RESOURCE *Publications* · Eugene, Oregon

THE IDEAL KING
Jesus in Light of the Mosaic Ideal

Copyright © 2025 John K. Grant. All rights reserved. Except for brief quotations in critical publications or reviews, no part of this book may be reproduced in any manner without prior written permission from the publisher. Write: Permissions, Wipf and Stock Publishers, 199 W. 8th Ave., Suite 3, Eugene, OR 97401.

Resource Publications
An Imprint of Wipf and Stock Publishers
199 W. 8th Ave., Suite 3
Eugene, OR 97401

www.wipfandstock.com

PAPERBACK ISBN: 978-1-4982-8910-8
HARDCOVER ISBN: 978-1-4982-8912-2
EBOOK ISBN: 978-1-4982-8911-5

VERSION NUMBER 072825

Scripture quotations taken from The Holy Bible, New International Version®, NIV®. Copyright © 2011 by Biblica, Inc. Used with permission of Zondervan. All rights reserved worldwide.

Scripture quotations taken from The Living Bible copyright © 1971 by Tyndale House Foundation. Used by permission of Tyndale House Publishers Inc., Carol Stream, Illinois 60188. All rights reserved.

I dedicate this work to my best friend and wife, Megan, and our children, Harper, Kennon, Jones, and Hudson. Megan, I am grateful for the King's good and perfect gift: you. May the King usher us into his kingdom and expand his kingdom through our family.

Contents

1 Jesus, the Ideal King | 1
2 Expectations of the Ideal King | 19
3 Really . . . Like the Nations? | 49
4 Where Have All the Good Kings Gone? | 80
5 The Ideal King | 101

Bibliography | 129

1

Jesus, the Ideal King

Introduction

"The King of Israel" was the placard placed above Jesus's head while nailed to the cross, a severe form of execution practiced by the Romans (though not invented by the Romans). While the sign may have been intended as mockery by the Romans, ironically, it wasn't. The truth of that sign, and Jesus's exalted place on that cross, spoke volumes about the King-God who was restoring cosmic order from chaos. The placard above Jesus's head rightly identified Jesus as the king of Israel and, more than that, the Ideal King.

The Jewish leaders found the placard insulting because those who saw the sign might think that man upon the cross represented the Jewish image of kingship. No true king of theirs, especially one claiming to be messiah, would be found on a cross. While there was no universal agreement on what the messianic figure might be, one vision of the messianic king was of one who would come in power—wielding swords, like David of old—and rid the land of the Romans, their imperial overlords. Jesus was not the king Rome imagined nor for which Israel hoped. But, Jesus was and is, in fact, a king, *the* ideal king. Jesus said as much in his conversation with

The Ideal King

Pilate. Jesus explained, "My kingdom is not of this world."[1] Within Jesus's words is a royal ideology we may easily miss without tracing the theme of kingship throughout the Old Testament. In Jesus's brief statement, he admitted his kingship and laid out his royal ideology—namely, his rule was not of this world. What on earth could Jesus have meant?

Throughout God's revelation in the Bible, few themes are more significant than kingship. Few themes have been written on more than kingship too. Yet here is another book seeking to dive into the subject of biblical kingship, particularly the nature of Jesus's kingship, how it aligns and fulfills the biblical ideal, and what it means for the twenty-first-century Jesus-follower today. This book is necessary because the meaning of Jesus's kingship seems lost on much of American Christendom. For example, In *Good Faith: Being a Christian When Society Thinks You're Irrelevant and Extreme*, David Kinnaman and Gabe Lyons document that 84 percent of Americans believe that "enjoying yourself is the highest goal."[2] At the same time, the majority of Americans identify as Christian.[3] It appears that a potentially large number of self-identified Christians have lost sight of the crucified Messiah, who came not to enjoy himself but to serve others. We need to rediscover the radical nature of the ideal king. We have a journey to take before we reach the ever-so practical application for modern Christians. Our journey will end at Calvary, where the most explicit teaching on Christ's kingship is clearly demonstrated.

Our first steps on this journey will include a preliminary investigation by tracing kingship as a theme in Scripture. Let us not forget the kingship theme originates early in the biblical account and remains central to the biblical canon until the New Testament canon closes.[4] Many passages in between those bookends of Genesis and Revelation speak of various royal ideologies, whether described explicitly or presented implicitly. However, these

---

1. John 18:36.
2. Kinnaman and Lyons, *Good Faith*, 34.
3. Pew Research Center, "Religious Landscape Study."
4. Gen 1; Rev 21–22.

competing ideologies only highlight the Ideal King, who pursued his people to renew and restore his broken kingdom, ultimately through death on a cross.

If this grand story is kept in mind while reading the Bible, then the whole Bible becomes a commentary on the nature of true sovereignty. Over against all the imperial[5] powers that rise and fall throughout the Bible's narrative, there stands one King and kingdom—centered not in coercive power, wealth hoarding, or political expediency, but in proclaiming the truth of a lost world sought out by its Creator and King. It is up to us to listen carefully to the story's narrative and observe where the meta-narrative is running. Where is the narrative running? To the cross.

The grand story is moving toward the paradoxical throne of Christ. At Calvary, Christ defeats the powers of this age and initiates the reconciliation process carried on by his vice-regents. Those who pledge allegiance to Christ are called to rule as Christ did through service and humility. We'll get to those texts in due time. Our first step, though, is to see how the Bible's narrative about kingship begins.

The Bible opens with God demonstrating his sovereign rule as he creates the cosmos, wisely ordaining and sustaining it. These chapters have received a great deal of attention from various creation-theory proponents, but these chapters are not concerned with explaining the *how* of creation but rather the *why*. We like to ask questions such as: Are these chapters really about the literal creation of matter about ten thousand years ago? Are the days literal twenty-four-hour days? Or, is there a gap between Gen 1:1 and 1:2? Maybe the universe is old, and God used time to bring nature

---

5. *Imperial* and *imperialism* are terms used throughout this work. I think it may be important to define exactly what is meant by this term. "State policy, practice, or advocacy of extending power and dominion, especially by direct territorial acquisition or by gaining political and economic control of other areas. Because it always involves the use of power, whether military force or some subtler form, imperialism has often been considered morally reprehensible, and the term is frequently employed in international propaganda to denounce and discredit an opponent's foreign policy." Editors et al., "Imperialism," para. 1.

where it is now. I suspect those debates will continue. Despite our preference for such questions, I'm in the camp with those scholars who say the whole "creation of matter" issue is not the text's focus. Something else entirely is the focus of those chapters.

Scholars have frequently pointed out how the poetic nature of the creation account in Gen 1 and 2 is not so focused on the creation of matter (the time, means, place, etc.), but the establishment of purposes and fixing of destinies. Here are two Old Testament scholars who offer this summary of Gen 1 and 2:

> The emphasis in creation in the ancient world—and the Bible—was *bringing order out of chaos* rather than *bringing something out of nothing or something out of something else*. That is why Genesis 1:2 starts with "formless and void" ["chaos"] rather than with nothing.[6]

Already, a key emphasis appears when considering biblical kingship. Kingship after God's image and likeness is a rule in which order comes out of chaos, where things move toward unity and peace, or shalom. When appropriate, we'll take a close look at David, supposedly Israel's greatest king, and see if he fits the ideal mold. However, before we leave Gen 1 and 2, here is one more Old Testament scholar on the primary purpose of those chapters, after examining critical Hebrew lexical data:

> In all of these cases something is brought into existence *functionally*, not necessarily *materially*; rarely would the statement concern the issue of matter. . . . The lexical analysis suggests that the essence of the word that the text has chosen, *bara'*, concerns bringing heaven and earth into existence by focusing *on operation through organization and assignment of roles and functions*.[7]

Walton again emphasizes the core of God's sovereign rule lies not primarily in his sheer power, albeit immense and impressive. Instead, God demonstrates his sovereignty through his ability to order chaos, assign roles, and bring about final unity. Not to jump

---

6. Hill and Walton, *Survey of the Old Testament*, 56.
7. Walton, *Ancient Near Eastern Thought*, 183.

to the punch line too early, but does that sound like Jesus? It's essential to introduce Scripture's major parameters on true, biblical kingship starting in the earliest chapters of God's grand redemptive narrative.

As the redemption narrative moves forward, God forms for himself a people who will be his unique representatives and heralds of his true kingship. His people begin as a person—namely, Abraham.[8] Abraham fathers a nation (and I am one of them, and so are you!). This birthed nation finds itself in a foreign land, Egypt.

As the book of Exodus opens, God's people find themselves in Egyptian slavery. After centuries of shackles, God hears the cries of his people and sovereignly rescues his people through incredible signs and wonders, all of which demonstrate his sovereignty over all things.[9] God takes the chaos of his people's slavery, their internal disunity, and their grumbling and brings about a unified people through which he will rescue the world. God accomplishes this task, frees his people, and calls them vice-regents in his kingdom.[10] These newly saved people become the subjects of God's kingly rule under God's chief vice-regent, the prophet-king Moses.[11]

Following his people's miraculous salvation from slavery in Egypt, God provides for his people as they move toward their promised inheritance, the land of Israel. Nonetheless, the people fail to trust the God who had just parted the seas along the way. The consequences of their rebellion include their wandering in the wilderness for forty years before entering the land and finding home. Moses leads the emerging nation throughout their years of wandering, and Joshua serves alongside Moses as his understudy. When we reach Deuteronomy, Moses gives his final speeches as the emerging nation encamps at the threshold of the land. Israel will soon enter the promised land, but not with Moses leading them. Joshua will take the lead of God's people, but not without Moses's divinely given expectations for God's chosen people's

8. Gen 12–34.
9. Exod 3–15.
10. Exod 19–20.
11. Exod 19:6.

The Ideal King

social, political, and religious framework. Moses's speeches include specific prescriptions for Israel's future kings.[12] Although the narrative to this point demonstrates that God is king over Israel (as well as the entire cosmos), Israel's vice-regents will function more like prophet-priest-kings, much like Moses. This passage, Deut 17:14–20, is of such importance to the trajectory of this study a chapter will be devoted to examining the regal prescriptions. Suffice it to say here, the expectations articulated are exact, detailing the restraints to be placed on the king as a reminder to both the king and people who truly reigns. Unlike the kings of the ancient Near East, Israel's king was to be singularly focused on knowing and embodying God's word.

The king God demands is so different from what the people are familiar with that the people initiate a coup d'état against God and install a king with the expectation that he will be like the other nations, not like the prescriptions given by God through Moses in Deut 17:14–20.[13] The result is disastrous. In denying the true reigning king, a disillusioned mindset came over the people. During the relatively short-lived existence of a unified Israel, followed by a divided people into Israel and Judah as separate nations, most of these vice-regents failed to meet their prescribed Mosaic requirements. The end proved catastrophic. As Assyria and Babylon took the northern and southern kingdoms of Israel to exile, one of God's prophets gave God's word to his people, saying, "Where is your king, that he may save you?"[14] The irony is striking.

Thankfully, exile was not the end of the story. A few centuries later, in about the fifth century BC, the people returned from Persian exile. They rebuilt Jerusalem.[15] A new temple is erected where the previous temple stood. Despite the physical exile being over, a theological exile still entrapped the people.[16] The people awaited the true king of Israel, the one who was promised to David's royal

---

12. Deut 17:14–20.
13. 1 Sam 8:4–20.
14. Hos 13:9–10.
15. Neh 1–3.
16. Wright, *New Testament and the People of God*.

line to enter Jerusalem and reestablish God's rule over his people.[17] According to the New Testament Gospels, the Fourth Gospel in particular, this true king—the one who fits the Mosaic prescription most fully, the one who came from David's line, the one who will concern himself with the law and not power, money, or political security—is Jesus.[18] And according to the New Testament, the canonical theme of kingship comes to its fulfillment in the central canonical character, Jesus Christ.

While the issue of kingship is essential in all the Gospels, the issue of kingship in the Fourth Gospel demands special attention. Kingship is a significant theme in the Fourth Gospel as Jesus's kingship is a substantial part of John's Christological portrait. In the Synoptic Gospels—Matthew, Mark and Luke—the kingdom of God is front and center; in the Fourth Gospel, the king, and not the kingdom, is central. While the Synoptics say much about the kingdom of God—or as Matthew prefers, the "kingdom of heaven"[19]—the Synoptics speak about the identity and role of the king half as much as John. Thatcher comments on John's Christology, saying, "John is so concerned with the identity and mission of Christ that the message *about* Jesus totally displaces the message of Jesus in his Gospel, at least those aspects of Jesus' message that went beyond statements concerning his own identity and status."[20] But a scholar might not have had to point that out to you. A simple concordance would suffice. Look at how often John uses the title *king*. John uses *king* sixteen times, which is more than any of the Synoptics, and each occurrence refers to Jesus.[21] The repetition of *king* cannot be overlooked.[22] It seems as if the Fourth Gospel

17. 2 Sam 7; Zech 9, 12.

18. John 1:49; 18–19.

19. Matthew uses this phrase thirty-one times and it is exclusive to Matthew (Matt 3:2; 4:17; 5:3, 10, 19–20; 7:21; 8:11; 10:7; 11:11, 12; 13:11, 24, 31, 33, 44, 45, 47, 52; 16:19; 18:1, 3–4, 23; 19:14, 23; 20:1; 22:2; 23:13; 25:1, 14).

20. Thatcher, *Greater than Caesar*, 5.

21. John 1:49; 6:15; 12:13, 15; 18:33, 37 (twice), 39; 19:3, 12, 14, 15 (twice), 19, 21 (twice). See Morris, *Gospel According to John*, 147; cf. Meeks, *Prophet King*, 18.

22. About biblical repetition, Alter writes, "The repetition of single words

is mainly concerned with the nature and identity of God's ideal king of his kingdom. John's Gospel demonstrates Jesus's kingship through word and deed.[23] One particular passage is essential to mention and is exclusive to John's Gospel.

Only in John does Jesus describe the nature of his kingship.[24] When you read Jesus's words he speaks to Pilate, one must ask where his kingship ideology is rooted. Jesus roots his conversations in the Scriptures, the Old Testament. So, where might Jesus have looked to in describing his kingship? Only Deut 17:14–20 contains an explicit explanation of Israel's ideal king. Like the Synoptics, Deuteronomy describes in detail what the kingdom is going to be like. But, like John's Gospel, Deut 17:14–20 focuses mainly on the nature and identity of the kingdom's king. The question, then, is which royal ideology in the Bible did Jesus understand his reign fulfilling if not Deut 17:14–20? Is there another royal ideological alternative? Or, did John's Gospel use the Mosaic royal ideology in Deut 17 as the frame in which the portrait of Jesus's kingship is hung? If so, what does that mean for Jesus's kingdom-dwellers, his vice-regents? Shouldn't our stewardship follow the pattern of our Lord?

First-Century Considerations

Before we embark on our journey, we must include an overview of the New Testament material on kingship for context. Kingdom is an essential theme in the New Testament, much like the Old Testament, although kingship undergoes reinterpretation because of Jesus. The way the Scriptures were interpreted underwent a

---

or brief phrases often exhibits a frequency, a saliency, and a thematic significance quite unlike what we may be accustomed to from other narrative traditions. The one most prominent device involving the repetition of single words is the use of the *Leitwort*, the thematic key-word, as a way of enunciating and developing the moral, historical, psychological, or theological meanings of the story." *Art of Biblical Narrative*, 181.

23. John 1:49; 2:13–25; 12:13; 18:33. See Wright, *Jesus and the Victory of God*, 490, 492.

24. John 18:36, 37.

JESUS, THE IDEAL KING

dramatic shift as the written word was enfleshed as the incarnated Word, God himself. Jesus's life, ministry, death, and resurrection were not the only reasons for scriptural reinterpretation, although they were paramount.

Other factors were essential to the scriptural reworking evident in the New Testament world. Though Israel is not in physical exile, their exile continued spiritually.[25] God seemed absent from his people. Israel was not under their own rule. A foreign imperial power ruled over Israel from afar. A foreign army was stationed in local barracks. A foreign currency filled the marketplace as the people awaited the coming messianic king and deliverer. But, what kind of king? N. T. Wright explains that the majority hoped for a messianic king who fit Davidic messianic hopes, which included militaristic means and defeating the imperial powers by imperial means.[26] Such a king would not come, however. There was another messianic vision, one rooted in the prophecies of the Old Testament. This messiah was not a military leader but a prophet-king whose sole focus was the Torah. This king was concerned most with shepherding God's people toward holiness, peace, order, and purpose. Compared to the kings in Israel's history, the king most resembling such an ideal was not David, Solomon, or Josiah. The most similar example was Moses. It was this messianic and royal vision that framed Jesus's kingship in the Fourth Gospel. Jesus's kingship followed (and surpassed) Moses's ideal kingship. After all, Jesus surpassed Moses in every way. As John uses Moses as a means of showing Jesus's superiority,[27] John's presentation of Jesus's kingship, too, is shown to be superior.

---

25. Wright, *New Testament and the People of God*.

26. This should not be understood to mean that the whole Jewish populace held one idea of a coming messianic figure, though it does seem the militaristic messiah was most popular. Fredriksen, *From Jesus to Christ*. Rather, Qumran shows the existence of a wide variance of messianic hopes. Wright writes, "Modern scholarship has made one thing quite clear: there was no single monolithic and uniform 'messianic expectation' among first century Jews;" however, that there were messianic hopes, albeit variegated, is firmly established. *New Testament and the People of God*, 307, 319.

27. Morris, *Gospel According to John*, 92, 100; cf. John 1:14, 17.

The Ideal King

Have modern Western Jesus-followers not considered carefully enough what Jesus says about his kingship? In each of the four Gospels, Jesus affirms his kingship during his interrogation by Pilate;[28] However, only in the Fourth Gospel does Jesus clarify what his kingship means. Whereas Matthew, Mark, and Luke emphasize the kingdom of God, only in the Fourth Gospel does Jesus give greater detail about his role as king. To put it another way, only in John's Gospel do we find Jesus giving his explicit understanding of his own identity as Israel's ideal king. How he defines his kingship is just as radical as Jesus's description of God's coming kingdom.

Jesus defines his kingship during his interrogation by Pilate in John 18:36–37. Within this passage, the function of the title *king* in John's Gospel "appears most clearly at the center of attention, in the trial before Pilate."[29] Since kingship is central to John's Gospel, how does John understand Jesus's kingship? How does Jesus define his kingship? Thatcher asserts John's Christology is inherently anti-imperial and most often negative, meaning John "says a great deal more about what Jesus is *not* than about what Jesus actually *is*."[30] In short, the real Jesus is not the Jesus of imperial churches or political alliances. The ideal king is found in the central Johannine passage concerning Jesus's kingship, John 18:34–38.[31] In that passage, Jesus roots his kingship in the Old Testament, precisely where the ideal king is prescribed. In John 18:34–38, Jesus alludes to Deut 17:14–20 by following the same pattern of discourse as in Deut 17:14–20, much the same way Philo, a contemporary of Jesus, describes the ideal in his *De Vita Mosis, I*.[32] While pieces of this interrogation are paralleled in the other Gospels,[33] John 18:34–38

---

28. Matt 27:11; Mark 15:2; Luke 23:3; John 18:37.
29. Meeks, *Prophet King*, 32.
30. Thatcher, *Greater than Caesar*, 11.
31. Meeks, *Prophet King*, 32.
32. Philo, *De Vita Mosis, I* 27.148–52.
33. For example, John 18:33 is paralleled in Matt 27:11, Mark 15:2, and Luke 23:3.

Jesus, the Ideal King

is unique to John.³⁴ This is another example of the Fourth Gospel's aim of presenting the nature and identity of the king, Jesus. What exactly do those statements say?

Jesus's statements present his kingship in two ways: first negatively (what Jesus's kingship does not include), then positively (what Jesus's kingship does include). Interestingly, this same pattern is used in Deut 17. For example, in Deut 17:16–17, three prohibitions are given concerning the function of the king: the king must not acquire many horses (build an army), have many wives (be concerned with political power), or gain much wealth (speaks for itself). Worldly speaking, these are normal pursuits for the powerful. But Jesus's kingdom is not of this world, and will not be identified by a powerful military or large cash on hand. Jesus's kingdom is different. Jesus is focused on the truth, much like Deuteronomy's king will be focused on the law.³⁵

Jesus's kingship is marked with his singular focus on the proclamation of truth.³⁶ If that was the king's mission, wouldn't it naturally follow that the king's subjects would do likewise? Are we, his followers, principally focused on the truth? Yet, how often are we enamored by things that are fleeting like the wind? Our pursuit of worldly, vain things is one way we demonstrate our lives are "like all the nations around us," which is emphatically not how the ideal king should behave. Jesus, in his own words, described his kingship this way: it was not of this world, as stated in John 18:36.³⁷ Our lives should also be not of this world.

34. Meeks, *Prophet King*, 63.
35. Deut 17:18–20.
36. Both positive and negative prescriptions (i.e., John 18; Deut 17) are linked by Philo who interprets Moses's kingship as the paradigm from which the positive and negative prescriptions came.
37. Philo writes, "Therefore, [Moses] alone of all the persons who have ever enjoyed supreme authority, neither accumulated treasures of silver and gold, nor levied taxes, nor acquired possession of houses, or property, or cattle, or servants of his household, or revenues, or anything else which has reference to magnificence and superfluity, although he might have acquired an unlimited abundance of them all." *De Vita Mosis I* 27.152. Philo was a contemporary of John's Gospel and Philo shows the belief in Moses as an ideal king was contemporary to John's Gospel. The idea that a king *could* be other than an imperial,

The Ideal King

The accumulation of power is the natural course of monarchs and rulers, much like the modern Western world. Yet, both biblical discourses say the true king is not to be like the nations or this world. We, then, as the king's followers, his vice-regents, are to rule in the same way. We cannot at the same time be rulers in God's kingdom while operating like all the nations. Christopher Wright's words about Deut 17:14–20 would also apply to John 18.[38] He says, "This text more or less says that whatever a king in Israel is to be, he is not to be like any usual earthly king, who enjoys weapons (military prestige), wealth (silver and gold) or wives (harem)." Now, apply that statement to Jesus's followers. Whatever "Christians" are to be, they are not like any normal earthly being who enjoys power, wealth, and pleasure. Sounds like Jesus, right?

You would think that amassing power is essential to maintaining rule. Somehow, Jesus's rule over the cosmos was finally realized, not through wielding power but through sacrificial love. During Jesus's passion, he did not attempt to stop the joke of a trial he was a part of. In John 18, Jesus was a king without military force preventing his arrest. Can you imagine a more other-worldly kingdom, one in which the king willingly demonstrates his love for his subjects through death? One way worldly powers sustain their power is through military might.[39] On the contrary, the ideal king was *never* to be a military figure. God was the military leader of his

---

militaristic figure was extant.

38. Wright, *Old Testament Ethics for the People of God*, 248.

39. In ancient Near Eastern imperial ideology, the most emphasized aspect of kingship ideology is the king as warrior, as in New Kingdom Egypt, for example. Kuhrt, *Ancient Near East*, 1:211. The same can be said for Assyria centuries later. Kuhrt writes, "The king as warrior is one of the most prominent aspects of Assyrian kingship." Kuhrt, *Ancient Near East*, 2:510. The similarities between the two imperial powers should not be surprising. The king as warrior was commonly shared among ancient Near Eastern civilizations despite their chronological place in history. Niehaus, *God at Sinai*, 299. Whether Egyptian or Assyrian, the ideal king stands diametrically opposed to the common ancient Near Eastern ideal. The same can be said of Rome. N. T. Wright writes, "Rome kept the peace by means of military might, crushing dissent and resistance with ruthless efficiency." *New Testament and the People of God*, 154.

people.⁴⁰ Moses, who actually established the pattern of the ideal king to come, was a shepherd, not special forces. Contemporary with John's Gospel is a belief that Moses was not a military figure, thereby fulfilling the ideal kingly prohibition of horses in Deut 17:16.⁴¹ John 18:36 says, "Jesus said, 'My kingdom is not of this world. If it were, my servants would fight to prevent my arrest by the Jewish leaders. But now my kingdom is from another place.'" On John 18:36, Morris writes,

> To demonstrate his point [that his kingdom is not of this world] Jesus points out that his followers are not engaging in any military activity. Had he been interested in what this world calls a "kingdom" a necessary first step would have been to recruit soldiers. His servants would be fighting men. But now, as things are, it is plain to all that he looks for no kingdom from this world.⁴²

Morris says the king expected by Jesus's contemporaries was a unique type of king.⁴³ Carter goes so far as to say that the lack of armed resistance on behalf of Jesus is *the* sign that his kingdom is from a different world.⁴⁴ Should the same be true for those who follow Jesus today? Should our lack of armed resistance show we are followers of Christ, trusting ourselves entirely to the God of infinite wisdom? Consider Carter's words regarding Jesus's kingship: "While Jesus' kingship does not present a military threat to Rome, it is nevertheless a real political threat to the way that Rome and Jerusalem order the world. His kingship participates in the completion of God's purposes, the establishment of God's reign/

---

40. Deut 3:22, 20:4.

41. Philo, *De Vita Mosis I* 27:148. (It must be admitted, though, that Philo makes no explicit mention of Deut 17:16.) "The horse was primarily perceived as an animal of war (Deut 20:1), hence the prohibition on a future Israelite king not to acquire great numbers of them." Alexander and Baker, *Pentateuch*, 917.

42. Morris, *Gospel According to John*, 680.

43. Morris, *Gospel According to John*, 521.

44. Carter, *John and Empire*, 303.

empire."[45] Christians pose a real threat to the way all the nations operate. The way of Christ is the way of self-sacrifice, love, simplicity, and truth. Jesus's way is opposed to the rampant worldly ways of self-promotion, greed, convenience, hoarding, and personal rights. Complete allegiance to the kingdom of God is what God desired all along.[46] The ideal king expanded God's rule without using military power, influence, or wealth. Today, the faithful follower of Christ expands God's rule the way he intended, through proclaiming and living the truth.

Why Jesus Changes Everything

Jesus is the centerpiece of Scripture and the interpretive key that unlocks the Bible. Jesus is the embodiment of the word of God, the fulfillment toward which the written word of God was pointing.[47] In John 5:39–40, Jesus says, "You study the Scriptures diligently because *you think* that in them you have eternal life. These are the very Scriptures that testify about me, yet you refuse to come to me to have life" (emphasis added). Reading the Bible is not about surface-level textual reading but reading that always returns to God's most apparent revelation in Jesus Christ. When considering what is true on any topic within the Bible, one must begin and end with Jesus. The Bible is a book that introduces us to the way of Jesus. It invites us to live, walk, eat, die, and rise with Jesus. Derek Flood writes, "The Bible was never meant to be a substitute for that living relationship with God. On the contrary, it's meant to lead us into that life-giving relationship. Scripture needs to lead us *into* this lived experience of the power of the gospel—causing our lives to be shaped by the gospel, so the gospel becomes *our* story."[48] The same is true when considering this topic of kingship and our vice-regency.

---

45. Carter, *John and Empire*, 302.
46. Deut 17:14–20.
47. Heb 1:1–4.
48. Flood, *Disarming Scripture*, 260.

Jesus, the Ideal King

John's Gospel calls Jesus *king* too frequently to be ignored, more so than the Synoptics.[49] John's connection between Jesus's identity and mission with the identity and mission of Israel's prescribed kings is one in need of significantly more attention.[50] John spends half of his Gospel on the final week of Jesus's life; it is worth examining more clearly why the term *king* occurs fourteen out of the sixteen times in John in these chapters. John's connection between Jesus's kingship and his passion week was intentional. If Jesus's kingship is intimately associated with his service, suffering, death, and resurrection, what does that mean for Jesus's followers? How does John use Jesus's final week to juxtapose kingdoms of this world with Jesus's kingship that turns the status quo around by being not of this world? Are we to live more like Jesus during his passion or like modern Western Christians? How does John use the trial of Jesus as the place in which Israel's messianic king not only testifies to the truth, but is crucified for doing so? And, didn't Jesus tell us we may well find ourselves in the same position when we fully and finally align ourselves with him? After all, Jesus is the goal toward which Jesus-followers are to run.

A Word About Methodology

My approach to this study of kingship will primarily be exegetical, with particular attention to the centrality of Jesus as the final and fullest picture of the biblical ideal. It may be necessary to address critical issues related to the biblical texts, though such issues are not the main focus of the study. The emphasis will lie on the

---

49. John 1:49; 6:15; 12:13, 15; 18:33, 37 (twice), 39; 19:3, 12, 14, 15 (twice), 19, 21 (twice).

50. A number of significant works in the Johannine scholarship say far too little about the role and identity of Jesus as Israel's king. For John, Jesus as king is central to the Gospel. Many authors mention the occurrence of βασιλεὺς as a theme, but they fail to go much further than this surface-level mentioning; see Köstenberger, *Theology of John's Gospel and Letters*; Morris, *Gospel According to John*; Thatcher, *Greater than Caesar*; Carter, *John and Empire*; and Meeks, *Prophet King*.

The Ideal King

intertextual interpretation of John's portrayal of Jesus's kingship in light of the Mosaic ideal.

Contextual issues, however, will be relevant. Royal ideologies were readily available in the ancient world. Already existent in Judaism of the first century is a belief in a coming king, though what that king was to be like is debated. As N. T. Wright points out, Josephus writes about messianic movements leading up to the Jewish War of 66–70 AD. About these events, Wright writes,

> What matters here is the fact that they existed at all: that under certain circumstances, reasonably large numbers of Jews would choose a previously unknown man (or, in the case of the Sicarii, a member of a would-be dynasty) and put him forward as a king, giving him a regal diadem and expecting him to lead them in a populist movement towards some kind of revolution.[51]

Other evidence listed by Wright will be investigated during the course of this study; however, suffice it to say the belief in a coming king existed in the first-century world. And, into this world Jesus came with a vastly different understanding of kingly power. It will be imperative to really understand first-century imperial power (and by connection to modern Western power) so as to best understand how other-worldly Jesus's reign really is.

Another royal image will need some examination. Jesus was a king.[52] He was also a shepherd.[53] The image of the shepherd-king is rather rich in history and biblical history. Moses was the first shepherd-king. Likewise, David was also described as a shepherd-king.[54] How does the image of a shepherd affect our understanding of Jesus's kingship? How do today's Jesus-followers act as shepherds?

N. T. Wright says, "If we know anything about the formation of Jewish belief and expectations in this period we know that it

---

51. Wright, *New Testament and the People of God*, 308.

52. Jesus is not only called king by individuals in John's narrative, Jesus also affirms for himself the title: John 1:49; 6:15; 18:34–36.

53. John 10.

54. 2 Sam 7:8; 1 Chr 17:7.

had a good deal to do with the reading of Scripture."[55] So, then, to Scripture we will go. Our intertextual study will seek to understand how Scripture relates the idea of the ideal king originally, how it critiqued various kings, and finally, how it presented Jesus as the ideal to which all his followers must adhere.

What exactly does intertextuality mean? Intertextuality does not just refer to one text building on a previous text; it also refers to the way the meaning of past and future texts "are also transformed or renewed by their embodiment in subsequent settings."[56] The Bible has multiple examples of royal embodiments, but only one earns the status as *the* royal embodiment, Jesus.

Final Thoughts

Jesus is the ideal king. Jesus is the *embodiment* of truth and the exact representation of God.[57] If we have seen him rightly, we see the Father.[58] Seeing Jesus rightly doesn't just affect our theology. Seeing Jesus for who he is will undoubtedly give us right thoughts about God and enable us to have proper theology. But, believing and thinking the right things is not why Jesus came. Seeing who God is will change how we live and worship. This is the ultimate point of this study. If this book contributes ideas or insights that are enjoyed and employed, well and good. But, if the study of this book changes hearts and lives to more closely conform to the image of Christ, the one who seeks and saves the lost, the one who is anti-imperial, who loves the poor and downtrodden, who is wary of wealth and power, who lives with absolute focus on the truth as revealed by God, then something worthwhile will have been accomplished.

The church cannot hide from the evil carried out by people claiming to be Christians. Yet, Jesus said we could tell whether

---

55. Wright, *New Testament and the People of God*, 310.
56. Soulen and Soulen, *Handbook of Biblical Criticism*, 87.
57. Heb 1:3.
58. John 14:9.

The Ideal King

people truly followed him or followed their own version of him. We are called to judge trees by their fruit.[59] Is the fruit we bear good for our neighbors? Are they in the image and likeness of Christ? Do the imperial, political, greedy forces at work in this world operate against Christians, or are we like all the nations, worldly and content? Jesus's manner of rule was others-centered. Our practice should be too. Jesus didn't expect power, wealth, or political savvy to usher in a better world. Nor should the church pursue power, wealth, or political power to usher in the kingdom. Jesus lived, walked, worked, talked, touched, and encouraged the lowly, downcast, and hurting. Jesus didn't entrust himself to mankind because he knew what was in each heart.[60] Jesus's entire kingly rule looked completely unlike all the nations. So should we. Jesus lays down how the new kingdom and new world will be ruled. Are we on board with his royal ideology? Do we know what his rule was like, and therefore what our following him means? We are to emulate Christ. It would do us well to carefully consider how Jesus was not only a king, or the king, but the *ideal* king. To what degree can we find a home in the imperial, greedy, political world of modernity and still be faithful to Jesus's other-worldly kingdom?

---

59. See Matt 7:15–20.
60. John 2:25.

2

Expectations of the Ideal King

What Makes an Ideal King?

THE BOOK OF DEUTERONOMY contains Moses's final sermons before his death, and before the Israelites crossed the Jordan and began settling in the promised land. These sermons are God's prescriptions for the newly formed nation. Included in these prescriptions is God's prescription for the ideal king, which Israel would seek out after settling in the land. The prescription for Israel's ideal king is found in Deut 17:14–20. The criterion expounded upon there serves as the scales on which the later kings are weighed.

In Deut 17, Moses, a shadowy forerunner of the ideal prophet-king, gives his final exposition to Israel before the Israelites pass into the promised land. Due to his disobedience, Moses will not make this journey into their new home but will only glimpse the promised land from a distance.[1] As Moses's last address to the nation before turning leadership over to Joshua, he prescribes for Israel how God expects the nation to live, and central to their way of life is what their future kings are to look like. As we listen to

---

1. Num 20:1–12.

The Ideal King

Moses's words, it will be essential to remember that Moses spent his formative years watching imperial Egypt at the height of its imperial prowess.[2] As an old man who seems convinced that imperialism pales in comparison to God's creative, ordaining, and unifying power, Moses hopes to guide this nation toward a government remembering who really reigns: God. This government is to function like prophets and priests who pursue justice, much like himself, not warriors, politicians, and lobbyists.

What is clear from Deut 17 is how the ideal king was to be utterly different from other kings. But, how exactly? What were the most significant differences between the Israelite monarchy and those surrounding nations, particularly Egypt, Moses's schoolmaster? After all, at the time of Moses's proclamations, Israel was just miraculously delivered (and by "just," I mean after forty years of wandering in the wilderness) from a land with a distinct brand of monarchs, the pharaohs of Egypt. And whether textual criticism places Deut 17:14–20 against the backdrop of Middle Kingdom Egypt or even late in Israel's history under Assyrian domination, the anti-imperial tone remains consistent.[3] In this way, Scripture continues to show its living and breathing nature. The anti-imperial message of Deuteronomy continues to proclaim a better way to us moderns today, and its claim sounds like this: Jesus is King.

Moses's prescription describes an Israelite king with both priestly and prophetic roles. The unity of these seemingly different roles into a single person, not entirely unlike the unity of the two natures of Christ, is a reminder of the unity in the original creation. Before paradise was lost, there was unity and order, purpose, and justice. The Israelite kings were to bring Israel into a harmony that was analogous to the harmony of the creation. This type of kingship was not like the nations Israel was soon to dispossess.

---

2. This statement is assuming a final-form reading of the biblical text and the Pentateuchal narrative.

3. Whether the date for Deuteronomy is the mid-fifteenth century BC or the seventh century BC under Assyrian influence, the anti-imperial tone remains consistent. For the imperial ideologies of both Egypt and Assyria, and their respective fits against the ideal Mosaic king, see Kuhrt, *Ancient Near East*.

Expectations of the Ideal King

The kings of other nations, like the Canaanites, may have had cultic or religious expectations, but their primary purpose was as a warrior and defender of the nation. Kings in the Assyrian or Hittite empires were seen primarily in terms of violence, whether in upholding justice or dismantling uprisings.

Understanding the role of the king in Israel is paramount for understanding the rest of Israel's history, and even the New Testament. Israel's kings functioned more like prophets and priests than military, imperial kings common in the ancient Near East. Since the purpose of Israel's exodus from Egypt was so that Israel may worship God by becoming a *kingdom of priests*, and a light to the world,[4] Israel's royal ideology functioned as another example of Israel's unique relationship with the Lord.

Expectations of the Ideal King: Deuteronomy 17:14–20

The time has come to wrestle carefully with how the Israelite king was supposed to rule. If we are to adequately understand how Jesus is the fulfillment of the Mosaic ideal, we must understand precisely what the Mosaic ideal was. Moses's ideal is recorded in Deut 17:14–20. Before we look at the text in question, let's set the context.

Our passage falls within the second of four major sections in Deuteronomy, following Harrison's outline of Deuteronomy. Part two of Deuteronomy falls in the section spanning from 4:44 through chapter 26, labeled the "Law of God." Before this main section of Deuteronomy, which seems to be the focus of the book, Moses recounts of the "Acts of God" (1:1–4:43) and then closes his oration with two sections Harrison labels the "Covenant with God" (chapters 27–29) and "Appendices" (chapters 31–34).[5]

---

4. Exod 19:3–6; Isa 42:6.

5. Harrison, *Introduction to the Old Testament*, 635–36. Another helpful structure comes from Gordon Wenham in which he divides Deuteronomy into three sermons and an epilogue. Like Harrison, Wenham places Deut 17:14–20 in the second section titled "Exposition of the Law." The context of

The Ideal King

Deuteronomy 17:14–20 falls within the section where Moses expounds on the Ten Commandments, Deut 12—26:19. In this larger section, Moses explains how to live out the Ten Commandments on personal, social, and governmental levels.[6] These chapters include expositions on the way Israel is to treat fellow brothers and sisters,[7] prohibitions against idolatry,[8] issues of marriage,[9] and war.[10] The Lord, through Moses, prescribed a society that mirrored the future kingdom more than the earth-bound minds of men. This is not to say that what we find in Deuteronomy is the way things *ought to be* now, meaning some sort of return to a Mosaic-era theocracy. Scripture should not be read in such a flat manner. Rather, the Bible should be read knowing that God progressively revealed more about himself and his plan through the ages until the final and full revelation of his plan and himself in Jesus Christ.[11] The *word* of God should be read through the interpretive key, the *Word* of God. We will revisit this theme more throughout the book, but it must be left here abruptly. Suffice it to say, Israel was to be markedly different in its outworking of faith in daily living.

The immediate context of Deut 17:14–20, chapters 16 through 18, includes prescriptions for other leadership roles. The ideals Moses prescribed for national Israel in the second part of Deuteronomy would be true for individual Israelites. Just as the nation of Israel was supposed to live and lead differently, individual Israelite

---

this pericope is firmly planted in the right way to live in God's kingdom. See Wenham, *Exploring the Old Testament*, 125. This approach also understands Deuteronomy as a unified whole. While debate exists concerning the exact composition of Deuteronomy, the final form is what is important in this study precisely because the focus of the study is not the Old Testament. Rather, the Old Testament is the flight path toward which we are moving, and the destination is the kingship of Christ. Critical issues, while not unimportant, are nonessential in this study.

6. Harrison, *Introduction to the Old Testament*, 635.
7. Deut 14.
8. Deut 13.
9. Deut 22.
10. Deut 20.
11. Heb 1:1–4.

Expectations of the Ideal King

leaders were also to live and lead differently. The leaders of Israel functioned more like shepherds or stewards who administered in the likeness of their Lord. For example, in the immediate context there are the expectations for the judges,[12] which state most clearly that judges are to "follow justice and justice alone."[13] Moses also denounces the worshipping of other gods,[14] addresses the administration of proper management in legal cases,[15] and explains the expectations of priests, Levites, and prophets.[16] Each of these sections highlights distinctives of Israelite society; yet all these distinctives fall under the one umbrella of God's revealed character. No place was given in God's budding kingdom for people to be concerned with their own personal agendas. Judges were not to accept bribes, but "follow justice and justice alone."[17] Could you imagine a society where judges were only concerned with true justice? Or, consider prophets. If a prophet proclaimed for God a message from his own mind, he should be put to death.[18] How often do we hear messages "from God" proclaimed to the masses that neither resemble God's character or kingdom in any recognizable way? The results are often tragic.

Several years ago, when my wife and I were living in Mississippi, I remember seeing billboards that had a message of impending doom, and there was even a date specified: May 21, 2011. The "end of days" was allegedly scheduled, and a particular "prophet" discovered a secret, revelatory memo. He announced the date widely. When May 21, 2011, came and went without a cataclysmic disappearance of untold millions of Christians, the "prophetic" message was revised to reflect that a "spiritual" judgment did in fact occur in May. Next, the final judgment of our space-time universe was to happen in October 2011. To the consternation

12. Deut 16:18–20.
13. Deut 16:20.
14. Deut 16:21—17:7.
15. Deut 17:8–13.
16. Deut 18:1–22.
17. Deut 16:20.
18. Deut 18:20.

The Ideal King

of Christendom, major ridicule was levied against the church as yet another "prophetic" message failed to materialize. The consequences of such prophetic measures cannot be easily quantified.

Other nations, such as Egypt and Assyria, expected their judges to be just and their prophets to speak truly, but the consequences for Israelite judges and prophets who misspoke or judged without justice was death. Unjust judges and prophets who promoted their own agendas were not only evil, but they adversely affected the whole people. Similarly, Paul told the Galatians that false teaching is like a little yeast that spoils all the dough.[19] Such deluded selfishness is a detriment to society. It speaks of pride and shows concern for self over concern for all. Selfishness and pride ruin God's work, not advance it. Selfishness breeds chaos because it makes every individual an autonomous kingdom, each with their own rules, power struggles, etc. God's plan was better; the society being established was to be in God's image and likeness, was to establish order, enact justice, limit chaos, and pursue purpose. Every role was to help promote unity, order, and purpose. Just as God brought order out of chaos, God's people were to bring God's message of order and hope to a world of chaos and despair.

Within the general context of other national administrative roles being prescribed, Moses gave the Lord's expectations for the ideal king:

> When you enter the land the Lord your God is giving you and have taken possession of it and settled in it, and you say, "Let us set a king over us like all the nations around us," be sure to appoint over you a king the Lord your God chooses. He must be from among your fellow Israelites. Do not place a foreigner over you, one who is not an Israelite. The king, moreover, must not acquire great numbers of horses for himself or make the people return to Egypt to get more of them, for the Lord has told you, "You are not to go back that way again." He must not take many wives, or his heart will be led astray. He must not accumulate large amounts of silver and gold.

---

19. Gal 5:9.

> When he takes the throne of his kingdom, he is to write for himself on a scroll a copy of this law, taken from that of the Levitical priests. It is to be with him, and he is to read it all the days of his life so that he may learn to revere the Lord his God and follow carefully all the words of this law and these decrees and not consider himself better than his fellow Israelites and turn from the law to the right or to the left. Then he and his descendants will reign a long time over his kingdom in Israel.[20]

The king Moses describes here might be odd to us, and such a king would have been odd in Moses's day too. The other-worldly nature of the ideal king is striking compared to the backdrop of other ancient Near Eastern powers. When placed beside the ideal king, Jesus, this prescription makes perfect sense.

The proclamation of Moses hinges on two phrases: "like all the nations" and "certainly place over you the king the Lord your God chooses." Moses says, "When you enter the land the Lord your God is giving you and have taken possession of it and settled in it, and you say, 'Let us set a king over us *like all the nations around us*,' be sure to appoint over you *a king the Lord your God chooses*" (emphasis added).

To understand the other-worldly nature of the ideal king, it is crucial that "like all the nations" and "the king the Lord your God chooses" are understood as antithetical statements. These two phrases are contrastive, not comparative. Moses seems to know this budding nation will look to someone for leadership, as they have looked to him for the past few decades. Moses also seems to know that this budding nation may well look to the nations around it for administrative guidance. It is precisely this reality that Moses hopes to nip in the bud. "All the nations" have kings that are not ideal kings functioning as the Lord intends. Exactly what "like all the nations" means will be addressed later. Suffice it to say, however, "like all the nations" and "your God chooses" are not synonymous. Evidence for this comes through the means by which Moses begins describing the royal reign of Israelite kings.

20. Deut 17:14–20.

The Ideal King

First, unlike the kings of other nations, the king the Lord your God will choose must "not acquire great numbers of horses." Strange, isn't it, that Moses would first mention horses? Moses is not objecting to horses because he is against the equestrian community. Moses has in mind the purpose of horses in the ancient Near East. Horses were war machines. The more war machines you can touch, hear, smell, ride, and train, the more likely you will put your trust in your ability to wage war. "In war, reliance on them [machines of war] encourages the king to feel that he is self-sufficient and not dependent on God."[21] Moses, who was an excellent student of the human condition, knew that fickle hearts may find it easier to rely upon something seen rather than on the One who is unseen. Moses, who was raised in Pharaoh's court, knew well the military power of Egypt; at the same time, Moses also knew the utter sham Egypt's power was shown to be against God, who controlled wind, hail, fire, frogs, locusts, flies, health, and finally life and death itself.[22] A trillion war horses could not split the Red Sea. God did. In Exod 14:13–14, in the sight of the massive Egyptian army approaching Israel, Moses encourages the people by saying, "Do not be afraid. Stand firm and you will see the deliverance the Lord will bring you today. The Egyptians you see today you will never see again. The Lord will fight for you; you need only to be still."[23] The psalmist declares in Ps 20:7, "Some trust in chariots and some in horses, but we trust in the name of the Lord our God."

The command against acquiring horses is intended to close off the possibility of Israel returning to Egypt, something explicitly forbidden.[24] If you recall, not long after the miraculous exodus *from* Egypt, the people begin losing faith in Moses's plan and begin

---

21. Tigay, *Deuteronomy*, 167.
22. Exod 9–14.
23. Cf. Josh 10:10–14, 42.
24. Block, in "Burden of Leadership," 266, makes this interesting connection: "However, with a single exception, in the Pentateuch horses are mentioned only in connection with the Egyptians (Gen. 47:17; Exod. 9:3; 14:9, 23; 15:19; Deut. 11:4; 17:16)."

longing *for* Egypt. Moses's prohibition against acquiring horses included a prohibition to returning to Egypt physically and ideologically. (Deut 17:16). Moses knew once the people started acquiring for themselves articles of war, the nation would no longer feel their need for God's protection, who, ironically, had just made a public display of imperial Egypt's war machine. Moses was afraid that if the people began looking like the other nations (i.e., amassing horses, etc.), they would start thinking like the other nations too.

You might think a nation not defending itself is crazy. Maybe so. Is believing that the God of the universe is able to defend and avenge his people unorthodox, anti-intellectual, or un-American? Maybe believing that systemic violence, power, and oppression will finally solve all human ills is actually correct (despite recorded human history seemingly saying otherwise). Is it crazy to think there are alternative ways of governing? Moses seems to think so. Jesus did too.

All the discussions about military power, justice, and evil are valid. Those conversations should take place, but only under the umbrella of the most pressing questions God's people must answer. To whom is our full allegiance due, God or man, the Sovereign or the state? For which kingdom are we ambassadors? Is our earthly or heavenly citizenship our clearest identifier? What if we slightly updated Ps 20:7, which was quoted above, and rendered the text, "Some trust in nuclear submarines and some in stealth bombers, but we trust in the name of the Lord our God"? Would we say, "But those things are necessary today"? Would the king prescribed in Deut 17 believe so? Would Jesus?

Moses prohibits a second staple of imperial power in the ancient Near East, wives. The next prohibition of Moses focused on not taking many wives. Royal wives played important roles, and potentially devastating roles as is evident in 1 and 2 Kings. Craigie, in his commentary on Deuteronomy, writes, "The purpose in acquisition of many wives would normally be political; a marriage to a foreign princess could add strength to a treaty with a neighboring state. . . . And implicit in the procedure of a political marriage alliance is a deviation from the one and only true treaty

The Ideal King

of the Israelite state, namely, the treaty that finds its expression in the covenant with the Lord."[25] Craigie nails it. He understands the prohibition served on multiple levels. On the political level this prohibition isolated Israel from forming alliances with the other nations. Yes, Israel was to be a unique nation, a nation set apart for God. But, why did such a status preclude political allies? Abraham Heschel writes, "Reliance on a world power meant a demonstration of the belief that man rather than God, weapons rather than attachment to Him, determined the destiny of the nations."[26]

Modern followers of Jesus need to be reminded of this biblical injunction against reliance upon worldly powers. Christians today have relied upon world power in countless ways, and each of those ways demonstrate what is believed at the core of our being. Do we trust our financial planner, our political party, or do we trust the Lord? Are we leaving the house armed with faith in God, or are we leaving simply armed? Will things finally improve when the right person sits in the oval office, or will the politics of the nations prove incapable of solving the human condition (again)? It is not hard to say the right things about where our greatest hope lies, or in whom we ultimately trust. But, only in our actions with our money, our safety, or even our politics do we see what we really believe.

For ancient kings, alliances by marriage were politically and spiritually dangerous. The practical prohibition had profound implications on their theology and purity. Scripture records devastating examples of the wrong wife's effect on a man, and by implication the nation. Solomon, to whom we will return later in more detail, had seven hundred wives and three hundred concubines. Either Solomon had a very loose understanding of what Moses meant when he said "not many wives," or Solomon knew, but did not care. The latter seems more probable. In 1 Kgs 11, the final chapter of Solomon's life as recorded in the Bible, the text says Solomon "loved many foreign women . . . his wives turned his heart after

---

25. Craigie, *Book of Deuteronomy*, 256.
26. Heschel, *Prophets*, 89–90.

Expectations of the Ideal King

other gods."[27] Another example is Jezebel and Ahab. While Ahab may not have been Israel's "Man of the Year," his choice to marry Jezebel had disastrous effects. She killed off the Lord's prophets.[28]

Moses's prohibition against foreign alliances by marriage was ultimately to protect the nation's singular devotion to God. The wrong marriage can destroy any hopes of a person's full devotion to God's kingdom. What was true for a nation in Moses's day was true for individuals in Paul's day. Paul wrote to the Corinthians that not just bad marriages can be spiritually hazardous. Paul, acknowledging his words are not commands from the Lord, but his own wisdom, writes,

> Because of the present crisis, I think that it is good for a man to remain as he is. Are you pledged to a woman? Do not seek to be released. Are you free from such a commitment? Do not look for a wife. But if you do marry, you have not sinned; and if a virgin marries, she has not sinned. But those who marry will face many troubles in this life, and I want to spare you this.[29]

The consequence of having a divided heart between the Lord and any competitor is serious for any person. But, if the leader of a nation is divided and then falls from following the Lord, it would follow that the entire nation would likely fall from following the Lord. Moses was the husband to one wife given from a fellow follower of the God of Abraham. She was a great blessing to him, even saving his life.[30] The right woman desires a man to lead them together toward Christ. A healthy, holy nation wants the same thing.

Moses prohibited an unchecked growth in military power and political alliances through advantageous marriages. Moses's final prohibition concerned amassing excessive amounts of "silver and gold." Jeffrey Tigay, an Old Testament scholar, offers two reasons for Moses's prohibition: "This clause would restrain the king from imposing heavy taxes, but in context its primary concern is

27. 1 Kgs 11:1, 4.
28. 1 Kgs 18:4.
29. 1 Cor 7:26–28.
30. Exod 4:18–31.

The Ideal King

probably the danger that wealth would induce the illusion of self-sufficiency."[31] The heartbeat of the ideal king is becoming more audible. Moses is prescribing a king not like the other nations. Rather, Moses envisions a king who is principally concerned with his people's purity and faith. The ideal king was not to amass for himself money or possessions. Why? That's what most kings do, but Israel's kings were not supposed to be like most. This king was not to be a burden to his people, but a blessing.

I love how Tigay puts it: "The danger that wealth would induce the illusion of self-sufficiency." Wealth and possessions have a way of creating an illusion, don't they? Not only might accumulating wealth foster self-sufficiency, but wealth might also cause the king to think more highly of himself than he ought.[32] In the New Testament book of James, James warns the rich about the dangers of wealth and the illusion wealth creates.[33] Wealth can corrupt the heart and make the wealthy a burden to those around him, not a blessing. The ideal king was not to be a burden. Daniel Block, another prominent Old Testament scholar, agrees with Tigay's assertion that the prohibition of accumulating wealth was for the people's benefit. Block says, "However, in the broader context of ancient Near Eastern monarchies and in the light of the concern that the Israelite king did not consider himself superior to his countrymen (v. 20), he probably had in mind primarily the accumulation of private wealth by imposing heavy taxes on the citizenry."[34] Both Tigay and Block affirm Moses's ideal king was not to be a financial burden on his people. Rather than unjustly amassing for himself wealth from the pockets of his own people, the ideal king was to concern himself with Torah and the proper administration of God's justice.

Could you imagine modern governments, leaders, and kings operating this way? Imperial, self-protecting leaders and institutions need capital and resources to carry on their work. Such

---

31. Tigay, *Deuteronomy*, 168.
32. Rom 12:3.
33. Jas 5:1–6.
34. Block, "Burden of Leadership," 268.

institutions burden the people. As the government grows, so does the burden. But when money begins to run out, where do you turn next? When money begins to dry up, you turn to human capital. Later, we'll examine 1 Sam 8 in which the prophet Samuel outlines how a bad king's administrative "needs" grow to require more than tax revenue, but human capital. As Moses forewarned, the Israelite kings will more and more act like the kings of the other nations, and in doing so, they will burden their people unnecessarily.

In some ways, the accumulation of wealth is a burden on the one accumulating the wealth. The more you have, the more you think you are able to distance yourself from the problems and pains of the world. Yet, no amount of money can forestall the oncoming of old age and physical decay, the erosion of relationships, or the daily internal emotional pain. Such a futile attempt to completely control life's circumstances can naturally lead to despair. History is filled with examples of people who have attempted to find satisfaction in this life, only to find this dream elusive and impossible to grasp. Some who experience this perpetual dissatisfaction with life see their life as ultimately meaningless, much like Solomon. In Ecclesiastes, Solomon wrote,[35]

> I said to myself, "Come now, I will test you with pleasure to find out what is good." But that also proved to be meaningless. "Laughter," I said, "is madness. And what does pleasure accomplish?" I tried cheering myself with wine, and embracing folly—my mind still guiding me with wisdom. I wanted to see what was good for people to do under the heavens during the few days of their lives.
>
> I undertook great projects: I built houses for myself and planted vineyards. I made gardens and parks and planted all kinds of fruit trees in them. I made reservoirs to water groves of flourishing trees. I bought male and female slaves and had other slaves who were born in my

---

35. Solomon is traditionally believed to be the author of, or at least an author of, Ecclesiastes. Since this work is dealing with the Scriptures in their final form, and most often following along traditional lines of understanding, Solomon is suggested as the author of Ecclesiastes. Critically speaking, the question of authorship is not yet certain.

The Ideal King

house. I also owned more herds and flocks than anyone in Jerusalem before me. I amassed silver and gold for myself, and the treasure of kings and provinces. I acquired male and female singers, and a harem as well—the delights of a man's heart. I became greater by far than anyone in Jerusalem before me. In all this my wisdom stayed with me.

> I denied myself nothing my eyes desired;
> I refused my heart no pleasure.
> My heart took delight in all my labor,
>   and this was the reward for all my toil.
> Yet when I surveyed all that my hands had done
>   and what I had toiled to achieve,
> everything was meaningless, a chasing after the wind;
>   nothing was gained under the sun.[36]

Solomon was fantastically wealthy. Wealth would give him a one-way ticket to perpetual happiness, or so Solomon thought. Yet, Solomon declared "everything was meaningless." Long before the first king reigned in Jerusalem, and long, long before Solomon fell into despair, Moses prohibited the accumulation of wealth for Israel's kings. Wealth became the poor, pitiful treasure—a substitute for what only God himself could be. C. S. Lewis, a writer and philosopher of the twentieth century, said, "God cannot give us happiness apart from himself. There is no such thing."[37] Moses came to know God as the supreme treasure far from the palace of his upbringing while he was a nomadic shepherd in the wilderness of the Arabian peninsula. There, far from the riches of Egypt, Moses learned that wealth and power are poor substitutes for the presence of God. And as we will see, there is a king who doesn't amass horses, women, or wealth, but keeps his eyes only on the Lord. That king is the ideal king. That king is Jesus.

At this point in our examination of Deut 17:14–20, a few themes regarding the ideal king have emerged. The Israelite king was not supposed to be like the other nations with a different political and theological orientation. The primary function of kings in

---

36. Eccl 2:1–11.
37. Lewis, *Mere Christianity*, 50.

other nations was as a warrior. On the contrary, the Israelite king relied upon the Lord to fight his battles. Kings of other nations accumulated many wives for political expediency; the Israelite king's sole alliance was with God and the Lord of heaven's armies. Kings of other nations saw wealth as their reward as rulers and warriors; the ideal king remembered the Lord was his own reward.

Moses prohibited certain behaviors for the king, but he also prescribed other behaviors. Israel's king was not primarily a warrior or career politician; rather, the ideal king was a humble servant of God who functioned more like a priest and prophet. For example, when the Israelite king took his throne he was "to write for himself on a scroll a copy of this law, taken from that of the Levitical priests."[38] In other words, this king was to have a copy of something only those in the cultic life of Israel was to have. That which is normally handled only by the priests—namely, this law, or the Torah—the king was to write his own copy. He was to read his copy of the law "all the days of his life."[39]

What precisely was Moses referring to when he referenced "this law"? What exactly will the king have a copy of? Is Moses referring only to the political and cultic regulations of Deut 14–17? Or, is Moses referring to his speeches being recorded in Deuteronomy? The answer to this question may be found in the frequency that "this law" occurs in Deuteronomy. Daniel Block finds this phrase and phrases closely associated to it nineteen times throughout Deuteronomy, meaning that, at minimum, "this law" or "Torah" is referring to 5:1b—26:19 and 28:1–68 and at a maximum the entire collection of speeches in Deuteronomy, including the song of Moses and his benediction to the tribes.[40] With all of Deuteronomy at his fingertips, the king had all that the priests had

---

38. Deut 17:18.
39. Deut 17:19.
40. Block says "this Torah" occurs in 1:5; 4:8; 17:18–19; 27:3, 8, 26; 28:58, 61; 29:29; 31:9, 11–12, 24; and 32:46; "this written document of the Torah" is in 29:21; 30:10; and 31:26; and "this written document," is in 28:58; 29:20. "Burden of Leadership," 269.

The Ideal King

for his own personal study for the purpose of leading his people in the way of the Lord.

Israel's ideal king was primarily concerned with establishing a just society, with the Lord's justice as its model. Torah in Deuteronomy is not just a law code, but a "function of Yahweh's gift of life to Israel."[41] The king's task was to concern himself first with this gift of life so he could properly administer that gift to the people he led in service to the Lord. "The administration of justice in Israel as an obligation of the people places it in the context of Deuteronomy's radical vision for freedom in service to Yahweh and a society that protects the individual from the tyranny of powerful hierarchies."[42] The king's job was to ensure there was no radical swelling of his power by being in constant submission to the law of the Lord, learning humility and wisdom.

It is rather difficult to think highly of yourself when you are constantly seeking the glory and love of one infinitely greater than yourself. By constantly studying the precepts of the Lord, arrogance and pride would remain at a minimum. The ideal king of the Old Testament was to practice what Paul would later tell his Roman readers: "Do not think of yourself more highly than you ought, but rather think of yourself with sober judgment."[43] A Christian leader who thinks of themselves more highly than they ought is "Christian" in name only. Whether one is a prince or a pauper in the eyes of the world, in the eyes of God, we are all recipients of his radical grace. When you consider the law's expectation of perfect obedience to the Lord, any reader of God's word, kings included, would come face-to-face with their own sins, prejudices, failures, and pride. The law of the Lord would keep the unfathomable grace and mercy of the True King ever before that person.

A man who seeks to lead the Lord's people would be a fool to attempt leading them on his own merits. "Blessed are those who keep his statutes and seek him with all their heart—they do no

---

41. Alexander and Baker, *Dictionary of the Old Testament*, 188.
42. Alexander and Baker, *Dictionary of the Old Testament*, 188.
43. Rom 12:3.

wrong but follow his ways."[44] What if the leader of a nation, more specifically a "kingdom of priests," was the "blessed" one who kept the Lord's statutes and sought him with his whole heart? What if that leader really did no wrong? What might happen with the nation? Allow me to use some sanctified imagination. What if the ideal king's oath before taking office included an adapted form from Ps 119:30–32: "I will choose the way of faithfulness; I will set my heart on your laws. I will hold fast to your statutes, Lord; do not let me be put to shame. I will run in the path of your commands, for you have broadened my understanding."[45] When we survey the kings it will be apparent the kings of Israel and Judah did not abide by Moses's command.

Ancient Near Eastern imperial ideology stands markedly different from Israel's ideal king. Sadly, the difference becomes almost invisible when the monarchy moves from an idea to reality. God's prophet-king Moses was rather clear how dramatically different Israel's way of life was to be from the surrounding nations. One of Israel's most significant differences was the expectations of her ideal king. Israel's kings were to function as prophets and priests who (1) kept their eyes on the Lord, (2) studied his law continually, (3) exercised his rule unlike all the nations, and (4) lead the people in life-changing faith in God to provide every need at every turn. Moses's prescriptions for Israel's rooted king were formed through his experiences as he witnessed the True King effortlessly humble one of the world's most powerful empires, Egypt, despite all her military might, political power, and wealth. The True King had power Pharaoh could only dream of. All of nature, and even life and death, obey the Lord God. After witnessing such awesome power, power that decimated the essence of imperial power, Moses

---

44. Ps 119:2–3.
45. Here is the original text from Ps 119:30–32:

> I have chosen the way of faithfulness;
>   I have set my heart on your laws.
> I hold fast to your statutes, Lord;
>   do not let me be put to shame.
> I run in the path of your commands,
>   for you have broadened my understanding.

understood Israel's greatest hope was not some religious version of imperial Egypt, but complete dependency upon the True King. Moses's ideal king, then, was radically centered on humbly doing God's will and proclaiming his word.

Many generations later there would be one who claimed to be such a king, one who was not a king by military power, political presence, or wealth, but a king who was singularly focused on God's power and gospel. That king, too, was not like all the other nations. He was crucified between two thieves, buried in a grave, resurrected to life, and enthroned at the right hand of God. In the two thousand years since his enthronement, empires have come and gone, yet the kingdom of God continues to advance. Why? Because the king of that kingdom is the ideal king.

Deuteronomy and the Other Nations

Now that we've examined the expectations of the ideal king from Deut 17:14–20, the time has come to examine the meaning of Moses's phrase "like the nations around us." Who were those nations and what did those nations believe about the nature of kingship? Because the historical debates about Deuteronomy's origin still remain open, the best approach for surveying the nations includes a number of empires across time in the ancient Near East. There are scholars who argue that Deuteronomy follows a Hittite treaty form that was widespread in the mid-second millennium BC, and therefore likely had its origin in the time of Moses. Other Old Testament scholars could be arranged who argue Deuteronomy fits an Assyrian treaty form from the mid-first millennium BC.[46] Since

---

46. A brief list of scholars who argue for a mid-second millennium date: McConville, *Law and Theology in Deuteronomy*; Niehaus, "Central Sanctuary"; and Kline, *Treaty of the Great King*. A brief list of scholars who argue for a mid-first millennium date: Weinfeld, *Deuteronomy and the Deuteronomic School*; Van Seters, *In Search of History*; Römer, "Deuteronomy in Search of Origins." The reality of both these lists—and many more scholars could be listed on each side—is the evidence suggests either possibility. The evidence suggests that it is at least possible the presupposed worldview of the scholar informs how he or she reads the evidence. In other words, what the scholar has already believed

Expectations of the Ideal King

the jury is still out on the origin of Deuteronomy, why not take a look at a number of imperial powers that may or may not have had direct influence on Deuteronomy, but absolutely had influence on ancient Near Eastern royal ideology?

Egypt is important because the final form of the biblical narrative, the form we have in the Bible today, suggests Moses's education happening in Egypt. In Egypt, what would Moses's education have taught him regarding the ideal royal ideology? Even if Egypt was not the background empire for Deuteronomy, Egypt's influence is significant to the worldviews of the ancient Near East. Imperial ideology was largely shared between Egypt and other ancient Near Eastern societies like the Hittites, empires from Mesopotamia, and Assyria. Against the backdrop of these imperial empires, the emphasis of the Israelite monarchy will become obvious.

To introduce the imperial ideology of the ancient Near East, one scholar describes, in the broadest terms possible, the royal ideology of the ancient world. John Walton writes,

> In the ancient world the king stood between the divine and human realms mediating the power of the deity in his city and beyond. He communed with the gods, was privy to their councils, and enjoyed their favor and protection. He was responsible for maintaining justice, for leading battle, for initiating and accomplishing public building projects from canals to walls to temples, and had ultimate responsibility for the ongoing performance of the cult. Beyond that, every aspect of order and balance in the cosmos was associated with the king's execution of his role, as is demonstrated in this list of the expected benefits from Esarhaddon's reign.[47]

The points of departure for Israel's king from other ideologies are evident in Walton's summary. In Moses's description, the ideal king was not the mediator between divinity and humanity like the other nations, nor did he commune with the gods or find special privy to

---

about the Bible and Moses may inform their examination of the evidence. The origin of Deuteronomy is inconclusive.

47. Walton, *Ancient Near Eastern Thought*, 278.

The Ideal King

their divine councils. Furthermore, the king was not ultimately responsible for the cult. Moses's king was not better than his brother. Yes, similarities exist. The differences, though, are most significant. Points of departure remind us how markedly different Israel was to be. After all, of all the nations, Israel was to be God's special possession, his kingdom of priests.[48]

Walton's summary was merely a summary. The ideologies lying behind the biblical narrative deserve attention as we consider God's ideal king and, subsequently, modern Jesus-followers' response to the Lord's ideal kingdom. The biblical significance placed upon Egypt demands the study of imperial ideology beginning with Egypt.

What was the royal ideology of Egypt like? What were the central features of Egypt's royal ideology? What was Egypt's brand of imperialism? These are big questions. Where to begin? Interestingly, we will begin with the most fundamental aspect of royal ideology, which also was Moses first prohibition! Pharaoh was the chief warrior. "The most emphasized aspect of kingship in the New Kingdom is that of the king as a warrior, excelling in his mastery of the important weapons of war, particularly the light, two-wheeled chariot drawn by a team of horses—a novelty in New Kingdom Egypt."[49] At the center of the king's job description was the expectation that the king be a fighter, a leader of the Egyptian war machine.

The Bible records the horse-powered war machine of Egypt flexing its muscle as they pursued the recently liberated Israelites. Yet, their horses were no match for the strength of the sea. Pharaoh, who released Israel after the tenth plague, had a change of heart, regretting letting them go. Exodus 14:5–9 says,

> When the king of Egypt was told that the people had fled, Pharaoh and his officials changed their minds about them and said, "What have we done? We have let the Israelites go and have lost their services!" So he had his chariot made ready and took his army with him. He

---

48. Exod 19:6.
49. Kuhrt, *Ancient Near East*, 1:211.

Expectations of the Ideal King

> took six hundred of the best chariots, along with all the other chariots of Egypt, with officers over all of them. The Lord hardened the heart of Pharaoh king of Egypt, so that he pursued the Israelites, who were marching out boldly. The Egyptians—all Pharaoh's horses and chariots, horsemen and troops—pursued the Israelites and overtook them as they camped by the sea near Pi Hahiroth, opposite Baal Zephon.

Here, only six hundred of the best chariots are mentioned, not necessarily Egypt's entire cavalry armament, with twelve hundred horses, and then charioteers at Pharaoh's disposal. That is impressive. Also, each of these chariots had "officers over all of them." With Pharaoh at the helm, the Egyptians raced after the Israelites, ultimately to their own demise.

Egypt was not the only empire to flex its muscle in the ancient world. The Hittite Empire, mid-fifteenth century to mid-thirteenth century BC, had a royal ideology rather similar to Egypt's, meaning it stood in opposition to Israel's ideal king. Being commander of the armies was central. History often shows the Hittite kings leading their armies into battle personally.[50] One reason the king was primarily a warrior was because war was necessary, not only for defense but to keep the economy going. Kuhrt explains, "Victories brought tribute pouring in, much needed manpower that could be used to extend and maintain the agricultural base on which the state rested, and land which could be given out to high-level functionaries, such as the captains of the golden grooms, members of the royal family and cults."[51]

What was true for the other imperial empires could be said for Assyrian kings.[52] The king as warrior was "one of the most prominent aspects of Assyrian kingship: it is the royal role most emphasized in the splendid narrative reliefs decorating the palaces and celebrated by the annals and other royal inscriptions."[53] Their

---

50. Kuhrt, *Ancient Near East*, 1:280.
51. Kuhrt, *Ancient Near East*, 1:280.
52. Kuhrt, *Ancient Near East*, 2:518.
53. Kuhrt, *Ancient Near East*, 2:510.

The Ideal King

cruelty to those they defeated has been etched into history where reliefs show the severed heads of enemies brought back so that soldiers might make a name for themselves.[54] Severed heads were not the only spoils from war. Their wages from war included wealth, materials for building and new styles of architecture, manpower for the work, and even strange animals and plants.[55]

Imperial Egypt's ideology has as its foundation military power. But, Egypt was not the only imperial power to emphasize military dominance. The Hittites, Assyrians, Babylonians,[56] Persians,[57] and eventually the Romans[58] all established kingdoms on military power. In the course of human history not much has changed. Imperial powers still seek to carry bigger sticks than their enemies. Against such a backdrop the contrast of Israel's ideal king shows most clearly. Israel truly was not to be like the other nations. Egypt certainly is not the only imperial empire whose security is based upon the ability to wage victorious war on opposition. The long line of empires from Egypt to present-day imperial powers have significant military powers. America, who once was *the* military superpower in the world, still bases a great deal of its security upon its military prowess. Yet, one must honestly ask whether military power is truly a good indicator of the power of an empire? Simply by stepping back from our present situation and taking a long, well-thought look down the corridors of history, it becomes evident that military power ebbs and flows like the tides. No

---

54. Kuhrt, *Ancient Near East*, 2:519.

55. Kuhrt, *Ancient Near East*, 2:518.

56. Kuhrt points out that "many features of Babylonian kingship and royal ideology have to be inferred, rather than being directly illuminated, by the surviving evidence" though later mentions the king's role as "protector of the realm from rebellion and sedition." *Ancient Near East*, 2:604–5.

57. Kuhrt, *Ancient Near East*, 2:676, 678. Persian ideology believed the king was a direct representative of Ahuramazda (the Persians' chief god) whose job was to ensure happiness for all mankind, maintaining perfect order, and "putting down commotion."

58. N. T. Wright writes, "Rome kept the peace by means of military might, crushing dissent and resistance with ruthless efficiency." *New Testament and the People of God*, 154.

Expectations of the Ideal King

nation, state, or empire has ever survived indefinitely. And, based on that history, wagering that no empire whose strength rests on the ever-precarious power of war will do so seems to be reasonable. These types of empires are all too common in the human experience. Power, particularly the power to kill, seems like such a strong deterrent against opposition. Ironically, it is exactly that power that seems to breed such hatred in the oppressed that it is not a matter of *if* there will be opposition, but *when*. Furthermore, what is so tragic about the human condition is how accurately the Bible has identified man's preferences for power. Moses wrote in Deuteronomy that one day the people in the land will want a king, but not just any king: a king like the other nations. History shows their request was a bad one.

Moses asserted that Israel's ideal king was not to accumulate horses, political power, or wealth. It is true the text never said the king could not have any horses (army), political alliances, or financial excess. However, the ultimate purpose of the king was not to protect his own empire and provide for his own people, but to do good for all Israel as a steward of the true king, the Lord. The ideal Israelite king was not to consider himself better than his brothers, and he certainly was not considered divine, unlike the kings of the other nations.

Divinity and kingship seemed to go hand in hand in the ancient world. The Hittite king became divine at death. The Pharaoh of Egypt, too, was considered divine. Kuhrt says, "The king's divine nature was reaffirmed repeatedly, through the cult of the immortal part of his nature, the royal *ka*, for which a special temple was built at Luxor so that it was included in the annual Opet festival." And later, "The cult of the sun, associated with the image of empire, is something else that became increasingly prominent in this period, with which the king, as the divine son of Amun-Re, was closely connected."[59] With the context regarding the divinity associated with the Pharaohs of Egypt, the final two plagues on Egypt in Exodus take on new meaning.

---

59. Kuhrt, *Ancient Near East*, 1:215.

The Ideal King

The plagues carry implications in both the physical and theological realms. In Exod 10:21–29, the Lord darkens the sun. In this plague, the Egyptians are shown that Israel's God not only commands the physical universe, but also is superior to Amun-Re and the Egyptian pantheon. Upon seeing the darkened sun, Pharaoh allowed the Israelites to leave, a change in official policy from earlier plagues. With the physical and divine light darkened by Israel's God, Pharaoh says, "Go, worship the Lord. Even your women and children may go with you; only leave your flocks and herds behind."[60] This was the first time Pharaoh allowed all the people of Israel to leave. Pharaoh had given permission for only the men to leave Egypt in Exod 10:8. That was the first instance where Pharaoh explicitly said "Go," giving them permission to leave Egypt. Before he had said, "I will let your people go," or "You don't have to stay any longer."[61] As the plagues destroyed more of his royal ideology, his willingness to do all that Moses commanded grew. However, his newfound willingness to let the Israelites go and worship God dissolved back into stubbornness.

After his heart was hardened again, God sent one more plague not even Pharaoh could handle. The angel of death took the lives of all the firstborn males. After this, Pharaoh gave permission for Israel and all her possessions to leave Egypt. Just as Pharaoh could do nothing about the blotting out of the sun, he was powerless over the blotting out of life.

Egypt was not alone in considering its kings divine. Hittite kings had divine status, but normally at death. The Hittites were an empire of the late second or early first century BC. Kuhrt writes, "The king was officially the main priest of all the gods of Hatti. He himself was not divine, although his relationship to the gods was exceptionally close. . . . Only when he died did the king 'become a god'—the standard phrase to express a royal death."[62] Assyria, though not considering their kings divine, did regularly give the

---

60. Exod 10:24.
61. Exod 8:8, 9:28.
62. Kuhrt, *Ancient Near East*, 1:277.

title "Priest of Ashur" to their kings.[63] While the god Ashur was the final ruler, much like Israel's belief that the Lord was the supreme ruler, Assyria considered their king the chief executive of Ashur. On the contrary, the ideal Israelite king was not an official priest, nor was he necessarily the Lord's executive. To be sure, the king's duties were "priestly" in that he was concerned with personal and corporate faithfulness to the Lord; Israel's king was the national executive, but the prophets, such as Nathan, Isaiah, or Jeremiah, brought the living words of the Lord to the people. Certainly, the ideal Israelite king was not a divine figure during life or at death. Israel's kings were one of the people.

Moses warned Israel about the dangers of kings accumulating wives. One Israelite king, Solomon, radically disregarded Moses's prohibition against marrying many wives, which brought catastrophic results for himself and the nation. After Solomon's death the united kingdom was ruptured into a northern and southern kingdom. Within a few centuries, both the northern and southern kingdoms were subjugated and exiled from their homes.

In the ancient world, wives were not usually the king's soul mate, or one true love, but often one of many women in a sort of harem, and these royal wives served various purposes. For example, in Egypt, royal wives were closely associated with religious rituals and female deities.[64] In the New Kingdom period of Egyptian history, pharaoh "always had a principal wife, and a substantial number of subsidiary wives."[65] Wives sometimes were part of the spoils of war. While history is unsure about the roles of Assyrian wives, it is certain Assyrian kings had several wives.[66]

First Kings 11 records the fact that Solomon's many wives functioned in cultic roles, though in a negative sense. Their devotion to their own deities turned Solomon's heart away from following the Lord. Moses warned about the dangers of a divided heart. These wives would come from varying kingdoms with varying

---

63. Kuhrt, *Ancient Near East*, 2:507.
64. Kuhrt, *Ancient Near East*, 1:216.
65. Kuhrt, *Ancient Near East*, 1:216.
66. Kuhrt, *Ancient Near East*, 2:526.

religions. Loving these women may also mean acquiescing to their religious beliefs. Following other deities is idolatry, and idolatry was forbidden in the Ten Commandments.

To summarize thus far, Moses's description of the Israelite king fits well with Egyptian royal idolatry as the backdrop. After all, Moses was educated in Pharaoh's court. The areas of significance for the Egyptian king—his military emphasis, his divine personhood, and his many wives—are areas contrasted significantly in Deut 17:14-20. Moses permits Israel to install a king that God chooses, not a king like the nations such as Egypt. Israel chooses the latter. Here's how Deut 17 fits with the rest of the Old Testament story.

Deuteronomy 17:14-20 and the Rest of the Story

Moses spoke prophetically about Israel's future desire for a king. What Moses foresaw happening in Israel's future happened. Moses said that one day the elders of Israel would tire from the ad hoc style of judges and demand a permanent solution to their lack of consistent, national leadership. What Moses foresaw comes to pass in 1 Sam 8. In this passage, the elders of Israel come to Samuel to make their request known. These elders seem to know Moses prescribed a king, but they seemingly failed to remember the particular prescriptions for the ideal king. Samuel, the prophet-judge who was leading the nation at the time, saw through the elders' desire for a king for what they really wanted. Samuel called this demand for a king "evil." Yet, if Deuteronomy allows for a king, why did Samuel call their request evil? Their motives were wrong. They wanted for themselves what Moses spoke against. They wanted a king like the other nations.

The elders' desire backfires with the first man in office, as we will explore below. Sadly, the second and third kings over united Israel do not align much closer to Israel's ideal king. Following the third king over united Israel, the kingdom irreparably split. Both nations' kings follow the faulty model of other nations, though some kings stand out as exemplars for proper kingship. Both the northern and southern kingdoms end up in distant lands back under the yoke of foreign powers. Yet, thankfully, all is not lost. During the downward spiral of the kings voices are proclaiming the words of the Lord. Some are harsh, but many are filled with wonder and hope. Wonder is heard in the Lord's unceasing love for his people. Hope floods the prophets reminding the people that though they have forgotten what it means to be the people of the Lord, the Lord has not forgotten his people or his promise. The Lord promised he would one day provide the ideal king as Moses originally prescribed. The ideal king would walk among the people, eat with them, and cry with them. He would live the way he has called his people to live and satisfy the longings of their hearts. He would repair the kingdom. He would bind the wounds of the brokenhearted, but not just of Israel. Healing would come for the whole world. If there is any question as to who the biblical narrative is pointing toward, look no further than the king who entered his city, not on a war horse but a donkey.

Deuteronomy 17:14-20 and the New Testament

There is no direct quotation or allusion of this pericope in the New Testament, but there is certainly a thematic correlation. Jesus is the embodiment and fulfillment of Deut 17. His kingship, following the model of Deut 17, contrasts directly with the kingship the Jews of his day had in mind and the imperial power of Rome, which had many similarities to the Egypt of Moses's day. In John 6, right after Jesus feeds five thousand, the large group wanted to make him king by force. Their rationale was that this man who had the power to take a tiny amount of food and feed thousands of people must also have the power to rid Israel of its Roman influence. The Jews wanted a physical kingdom again, much like the Davidic period, or the more recent Maccabean period. However, this was not Jesus's intention.

Jesus did not come to make a name for himself. Rather, Jesus,

The Ideal King

> Who, being in very nature God, did not consider equality with God something to be used to his own advantage, rather made himself nothing, taking the very nature of a servant, being made in human likeness. And being found in appearance as a man, he humbled himself by becoming obedient to death—even death on a cross! Therefore God exalted him to the highest place and gave him the name that is above every name, that at the name of Jesus every knee should bow, in heaven and on earth and under the earth, and every tongue acknowledge that Jesus Christ is Lord, to the glory of God the Father.[67]

As this text shows, he submitted to the will of his Father. He was not about his own glory. As a result, he now holds the highest place with the name above every other name, the name at which every knee will bow and tongue confess that Jesus is Lord. He did not acquire horses, wives, or silver and gold. He came for those whom the Father had given him from eternity past.

Jesus describes the nature of his kingship in his conversation with Pilate. In John 18:36-37, "Jesus said, 'My kingdom is not of this world. If it were, my servants would fight to prevent my arrest by the Jews. But now my kingdom is from another place.' 'You are a king, then!" said Pilate. Jesus answered, 'You are right in saying I am a king. In fact, the reason I was born and came into the world is to testify to the truth. Everyone on the side of truth listens to me.'" When Jesus admits his kingship, he does so by saying this is why he came as a king, to testify to the truth, and those who are on the side of truth listen to Jesus. This is significant because it draws to mind the parallel with Deut 17:18-20. Moses said the true king would concern himself primarily with the Torah. Likewise, Jesus's kingship was focused on that same theme, albeit under a different name, *truth*. Jesus not only spoke the truth, but he was the truth.[68] Also fulfilling Deut 17:14-20, Jesus did not have too many horses or wives. His life was focused on faithfulness to God, which was the expectation of the ideal king in Deut 17. Jesus is

---

67. Phil 2:6-11.
68. John 14:6.

the king Moses described in Deut 17:14–20, and the only one ever capable of living up to the perfect standard needed to live the Deut 17:14–20 standards.

Conclusion

Deuteronomy 17:14–20 described the expectations of the Israelite monarchy. Juxtaposed against Egyptian royal ideology, it is easy to see the marked differences. The Israelite king did not function as a king in the ancient Near Eastern definition. New Kingdom Egypt royal ideology understood their kings to be excellent warriors and the sole protectors of Egypt. The Pharaohs were divine beings, as were some of their many wives. In contrast, God ruled Israel. God fought Israel's battles. God was who they were to worship only and he was their reward. The king functioned more like a priest and prophet. Wenham agrees. He says, "The king sounds more like a priest or a prophet than a secular ruler. All of them are responsible for making sure the nation does not adopt the magic practices of the Canaanites.[69] In other words all the authorities in Israel must be on their guard against allowing foreign worship to pollute national life."[70] The king's role in the maintenance of Israel's purity was to write his own copy of the law. It was his duty to know the law and live it, not turning to the right or to the left. In doing so, as the figurehead of Israel, the nation would follow. They would know God was the true king because their king believed himself to be the people's equal. The king's focus was on the Torah. Concerning every other matter, God was in control.

This role was not fulfilled by any human king ultimately because our human nature would most certainly be drawn away from God after easy access to money, sex, and power. Were we installed as kings, we would think ourselves better than our brothers and sisters and widen the gap between the elite and working class. Our fallen nature could not handle the responsibility, as evidenced

---

69. Deut 18:9–14.
70. Wenham, *Exploring the Old Testament*, 136.

by the kings of Israel. However, thanks be to God for Jesus who was concerned with truth only. He came to do the will of his Father and as king, he died for his people. Now, we are coheirs with him because he who knew no sin became sin for us, so that we might become the righteousness of God.[71]

---

71. Rom 8:17; 2 Cor 5:21.

3

Really . . . Like the Nations?

There Was No King In Israel

DEUTERONOMY RECORDS MOSES'S FINAL acts of leadership, in word and deed, before the nation he led for decades crossed the Jordan under new leadership. Moses, who functioned over Israel like the king he prescribed in Deut 17, chose Joshua as his successor. Once Israel established itself in the promised land, the work of kingdom building was to begin. And, as the kingdom grew, and the demand for a king emerged, Moses had prescribed the proper limits of the ideal king. Yet, Israel wandered from this prescription after the unsuccessful conquest of Israel under Joshua, Moses's successor.

Joshua began the conquest of Israel, but did not complete the mission. When Joshua's time to return to the earth comes, he, like Moses, gives a passionate plea to his people to singular devotion to the Lord God. Yet, his plea falls on deaf ears. After Joshua dies, a series of ad hoc judges are called upon to deliver Israel from their love of self and the sin that entraps them. As a result of this sin, the nation is in turmoil, often in subjugation to an enemy nation. These judges serve till death. After these judges die, Israel has

The Ideal King

peace for a short time, but then they return to their past enslaving sins and find themselves again under the yoke of an enemy power. The people are clearly aware of the need for a more permanent solution. Sadly, it does not cross the leaders' minds that maybe a devoted return to the Lord might be best. They think they want a monarchy just like all the nations. There is a chilling line in Judg 21:25: "In those days Israel had no king; everyone did as he saw fit."

Whoever wrote Judges showed a brilliant ability in writing on multiple levels. Yes, Israel was not yet a unified nation under a king. But, far more important than a physical king, as the author astutely points out, was the fact that the people no longer had *any* king, including the Lord himself, and as a result were doing as they saw fit. We will see shortly that merely having a man on the throne does not stop everyone doing as they see fit. Only the ideal king can do that. God foresaw Israel demanding a king, but not an ideal king. After the unsuccessful conquest of the promised land, and the repeating cycle of failure throughout the book of Judges, the time came for the "stability" of a monarchy. First Samuel 8:4 records the moment when "all the elders of Israel" demanded a worldly king from Samuel. The day the leaders made the ironic demand was really the beginning of the end for Israel because their request for a king was evil.

The books of Samuel are where the transition from ad hoc judges to the institutionalized monarchy occurs. Samuel is the prophet, priest, and judge who plays the pivotal role of bringing the people through this transition. Samuel functions as the last judge of Israel and also as the king maker. The importance of these books for the history of the Israelite monarchy, not to mention this book, is difficult to overemphasize.

Within the narrative of the books of Samuel are important stories like the institution of Israel's first king, the rise and reign of David, the transition from David to Solomon, the splitting of the kingdom after Solomon's demise, the rather rapid fall of the Northern Kingdom led by wicked kings, the slower, but still quick fall of the Southern Kingdom led predominantly by bad kings (but with a few bright spots along the way), and the final collapse and

Really ... Like the Nations?

exile of both kingdoms. Within these major stories are other major stories, but the general trajectory concerns kingship.

The main theme of 1 and 2 Samuel is found in the passage we will examine more carefully below: "But they have rejected me as king."[1] Irony? The people demand a king, a king like all the nations, yet they already abandoned the king greater than all the nations' kings combined. The concept that Israel's demand for a king is the rejection of the Lord occurs six more times between chapters 8 and 16. The author[2] of 1 Samuel emphasizes this rejection a number of times. The author writes, "You have not kept the Lord's command,"[3] and, "An evil thing you did in the eyes of the Lord

---

1. 1 Sam 8:7.
2. The authorship of 1 Samuel is difficult to ascertain. First Samuel offers no conclusive evidence internally as to who penned the book. First Samuel 10:25 records the Lord's command to Samuel to write the laws of the king down on a scroll. With this verse it seems plausible that Samuel writes at least a portion of this text during his many years as a leader at Mizpah. The portions that are believed to be possible from Samuel are the ark narrative (4:1—7:1), which is included in the larger section of the story of Samuel (1–7) and the crux of the corpus, 1 Sam 8. It is also possible that Samuel may have written the accounts of Saul (9–15), though material following this is likely from the Davidic era due to the content. The story of Saul and David (16–31), which deals with the tension and contrast between Saul, the now rejected king of Israel, and David, God's newly anointed heir, was probably composed during the early part of David's era when David still needed to justify his kingship. Considering that the death of Samuel is recorded in 1 Sam 25, the rest of the Samuel corpus that bears his name must be the product of a later editor. Tsumura, *First Book of Samuel*, 31.

The date, like authorship, is hard to determine with certainty. Following a traditionally conservative dating, sometime during the tenth century BC is suggested. Since the kingdom split in 930 BC, there would have to be time for the kingship of Solomon, David, and Saul. According to 1 Sam 13:1, Saul reigned over Israel for forty-two years. David reigned for forty years (2 Sam 5:4) and Solomon reigned forty years (2 Sam 11:42). So, according to the text and beginning with the split of the kingdom in 930 BC and working backward, adding the various reigns of Solomon, David, and Saul places a date of Saul's reign approximately at 1050 BC. The text says that when Saul was anointed as king, Samuel was an old man so then the earliest portions of the book can be written no earlier than the birth of Samuel in approximately 1109 BC.

3. 1 Sam 13:14.

The Ideal King

when you asked for a king."[4] From the outset the monarchy fails as it was initiated by the people's evil desire to be like the surrounding nations[5] rather than God's holy nation.[6] However, in contrast, a running theme throughout the book is also the faithfulness of the Lord. Yes, Israel has rejected her God, but her God has not rejected her. He will rescue Israel and, one day, the ideal king will rule with perfect justice and grace.

Lest we forget, kings were promised to Jacob in Gen 35.[7] Having a king is not the issue. Furthermore, as we examined in chapter 2, Moses provided the expectations of a king in Deut 17. As we continue our investigation, we might find evidence that Moses, not David, represented the closest example of the ideal king. No one will compare to Christ, who perfectly fulfills all the prescriptions of the ideal king. The real issue in 1 Sam 8 is the people's desire for the king so they can be like the other nations.[8]

Can we really judge them, though? Of course not. According to 1 Samuel, the leaders of ancient Israel had the same worldly tendencies. If you look around at contemporary Christendom, particularly our Protestant traditions, you will readily notice our worldliness. For example, our worship centers look, feel, and sound just like contemporary rock concerts. If the world produces screamo rock music and it sells, then we Christians absolutely produce the same thing except our screamos are screaming "JESUS." We forget just how countercultural the kingdom of God really is.

One more thing is needed before we turn to 1 Sam 8. What are the immediate factors contributing to Israel's demand for a king? What are the people facing that causes them to prefer a human king, one like the other nations as opposed to the Lord of heaven and earth?

---

4. 1 Sam 12:17.
5. 1 Sam 8:5.
6. Exod 19:6.
7. Gen 35:11.
8. 1 Sam 8:5.

REALLY . . . LIKE THE NATIONS?

The Coup d'État Against the Divine

Satterthwaite and McConville divide 1 Samuel into three larger portions, like a three act play, with 1 Sam 8 concluding act one and initiating act two.[9] The first act includes 1 Sam 1–7 covering Samuel's rise and Eli's demise. Also included in this section is the ark narrative,[10] which is understood to be among the oldest compositions in Samuel, possibly from a source contemporary with Samuel.[11] The next section is 8–15, which describes Saul's ascension to the throne and his reign. Here, I would make a contribution to Satterthwaite and McConville's divisions. First Samuel 8 does more than simply begin to tell of Saul's ascension to the throne. When looked at from cruising altitude, seeing not just a tree, but an entire forest, this chapter begins the story of Israel's exile. Israel takes another step away from God by acting contrary to his expressed will. Though kingship per se is not the issue, from the outset the monarchy is doomed. Why? The kings Israel desires look nothing like the king God requires. For this reason, I believe, 1 Sam 8 is the beginning of the end for the Israelite monarchy.

Turning now specifically to our passage, 1 Sam 8:4–9 concludes the first seven chapters. As stated above, 1 Samuel opens as the period of the judges comes to an end. Following the story of the birth of Samuel and his dedication,[12] evil and corruption are discovered in the Elite priesthood. The evil of Eli's sons Hophni and Phinehas is juxtaposed with the purity of Samuel,[13] and the result of their sin, which is ultimately a reflection on their father, Eli,[14] is the removal of the Elite priesthood and the initiation of God's anointed.[15]

---

9. Satterthwaite and McConville, *Exploring the Old Testament*, 105.
10. 1 Sam 4:1—7:1.
11. Tsumura, *First Book of Samuel*, 12.
12. 1 Sam 1:1—2:11.
13. 1 Sam 2:17–18.
14. 1 Sam 2:27–29.
15. 1 Sam 2:30–35.

The Ideal King

After the account of Samuel's election in chapter 3, the judgment pronounced against Eli has implications for the nation. Israel's army suffers a devastating loss to the Philistines. Eli hears the report like this: "Israel fled before the Philistines, and the army has suffered heavy losses. Also your two sons, Hophni and Phinehas, are dead, and the ark of God has been captured."[16] See the progression? The report gets worse as the servant retells the event and culminates in the death of his sons and the ark of the Lord being taken. Upon hearing this, Eli falls from his chair and dies. Chapter 4 ends with this depressing summary statement: "The Glory has departed from Israel."[17] Note, however, Israel's army lost, not God. The text turns to tell what happened to the ark after its capture.[18] The ark was returned to Israel and eventually rested in Kiriath Jearim for a period of twenty years.[19]

At this point in the narrative, the focus moves to Samuel. This chapter functions like a resume. The account opens with Samuel's call to repentance and removal of the false images of worship[20] followed by an account of deliverance from the Philistines.[21] The chapter closes with a summary statement of Samuel's leadership. He led Israel for forty years, and during his lifetime he delivered the Israelites from the hand of the Philistines and brought peace with the Amorites.[22] However, the constant threat of war weighed heavily on the Israelites. This anxiety causes them to panic. Their panic causes them to make a poor decision and initiate a coup d'état against Israel's divine king.

If space were to allow, it would be possible to trace this movement away from divine kingship beginning shortly after the people were led out of Egypt.[23] It is mind blowing how people could

---

16. 1 Sam 4:17.
17. 1 Sam 4:21.
18. 1 Sam 5:1—7:1.
19. 1 Sam 7:1–2.
20. 1 Sam 7:3–5.
21. 1 Sam 7:10–11.
22. 1 Sam 7:13–14.
23. Exod 16:3.

witness such miraculous events against an imperial power by God himself and then within a short period of time truly believe an imperial government is best. How quick we are to forget the truth and rely on our fickle feelings. Listen to Christians today who believe if the right person is elected to office, the nation will be okay. Or, if certain bills are passed, then all will be well. The systemic problem is much, much deeper than who is in office or what is deemed legal or illegal. The root problem is a problem of the soul and its disordered loves. We desire conformity to the standards of the world, not the standards of God and his kingdom. The ideal king has always been diametrically opposed to all the nations, and this difference will only become sharper when *the* ideal king arrives, Jesus.

We Demand a King

How did the coup begin? Simple. The elders of Israel who wanted a king, like all the nations, gathered themselves in one place, without Samuel present, to get their demands straight. Once consensus was reached, the elders went together to Samuel to demand. It is important to understand this minor detail in the passage. The elders were not weighing pros and cons, but had already decided they wanted what the other nations had, a physical, warrior king. Grass is always greener, right? The text says the elders "gathered together" and they "came."[24] Those two action verbs are linked, suggesting maybe the elders either spent little or no time in their deliberation about a king. The people are together in their desire. In their minds, a human king was in, God was out.

When the elders get to Samuel at Ramah, they say, "You are old, and your sons do not follow your ways; now appoint a king to lead us, such as all the other nations have."[25] Their demand is short, and with all the elders there Samuel sees a united front. First, the elders comment on Samuel's age. This is no slight, but reality. At

24. 1 Sam 8:4.
25. 1 Sam 8:5.

some point, Samuel will not be able to lead Israel anymore, so they want a permanent solution. And, they do not want Samuel's sons because they "do not follow your ways." Do you see the irony here?

The people want a king, like all the other nations, which includes royal succession. They do not have the benefit of all the historical inquiry and archaeological finds that paint a rather bleak picture of imperial kings and their royal lines. But, they do have one important piece of evidence right in front of them. They see that father-son succession may not always work. They see how possible it is to have the Lord's anointed have wicked children. They are standing in front of evidence suggesting their desired king is set up for failure. And, as we will see shortly, such familial succession rarely works to the advantage of the people. Deuteronomy 17:15 says, "Be sure to appoint over you a king the Lord your God chooses." The people choose a king based upon externals, not character. The Lord sees the heart. It will not be long until the people's inability to choose wisely comes back upon them. On top of that, the Lord's choice may not always be the son of a ruling king.

The elders of Israel wanted a particular king. Their hope was to have a king like all the nations, the identical phrase Moses used in Deuteronomy where Moses explains how drastically different the ideal king was to be from the nations. Maybe this is a case of bad biblical interpretation, a biblicism of the most dangerous sort. What if the elders of Israel knew their Bibles, chapter and verse? What if they knew the inspired words contained a promise of future kingship? And, in their knowledge of chapter and verse, and their understanding of every word being inspired, they lunged forth toward Samuel demanding a king because the Bible says so? I find this remarkably plausible, albeit not necessarily in the text before us. These people, as well as us modern Jesus-followers today, need a proper interpretive key to Scripture. What is that key? Not texts, but character. Not just any character, but the Character, Christ. Proper interpretation of Scripture must conform first to the character of God revealed in Christ. For those before the advent of Christ, their interpretive key was still to be God's character as evident in the expectations he laid on his people.

Really . . . Like the Nations?

Remember our study of Deut 17 concluded that the ideal king's external actions were an outpouring of the inward, fully God-reliant character. This person saw God's ability to provide in every circumstance. Enemy army invading? God defeated the most powerful empire on the face of the earth by simply speaking. God did not have to get out of his seat to fight. He did it once, and he can do it again. Feeling politically alone, isolated, and fearing destruction? No need. God, who made all things by the word of his mouth, is the only political alliance you need. Almost out of money? God, the author of life, feeds and cares for every animal, plant, and person. Live the way he prescribes and watch how needs are miraculously met. Such a person, one whose main focus is loving, learning, and practicing the law of God, practicing the character of God, is the one to lead the nation.

The elders' desire for a king was complex. Christopher Wright suggests, "The demand for a king sprang from a mixture of motives, some apparently good (the desire for justice and non-corrupt leadership, in the context of the embarrassing failure of Samuel's sons to provide it), others unquestionably retrograde (the desire to be like the rest of the nations)."[26] There's a world of difference between the two motives.

Samuel read between the lines. First Samuel 8:6 says, "But when they [the elders] said, 'Give us a king to lead us,' this displeased Samuel; so he prayed to the Lord." I try to bring as little of the original language into this book as possible so as not to imply that one *must* know the original language to really know Scripture and therefore all non-language learners will only have veiled access to Jesus. I once had a professor at seminary who said never to use Greek and Hebrew words from the pulpit because it can imply people cannot really get what they need from the Bible unless those languages are known. He strongly encouraged his students to make sure every observation can be made from the English text. However, I find this situation one where I must appreciate but disregard his advice. Here's why. Where the NIV says "displeased," the original Hebrew is *raa*, which means "evil." Literally, the text says

---

26. Wright, *Old Testament Ethics*, 230.

The Ideal King

Samuel understood their request to be "evil when they said, 'Give to us a king to judge us like all the other nations.'"[27]

Why was Samuel displeased? Or, literally, what did Samuel believe to be evil? Samuel knew what was really going on in their request. Samuel knew this request was tantamount to a royal overthrow. This interpretation is confirmed when Samuel prays to the Lord and the Lord speaks, saying in 1 Sam 8:7–9:

> Listen to all that the people are saying to you; it is not you they have rejected, but they have rejected me as their king. As they have done from the day I brought them up out of Egypt until this day, forsaking me and serving other gods, so they are doing to you. Now listen to them; but warn them solemnly and let them know what the king who will reign over them will claim as his rights.

Samuel knew the people demanded a grave evil. Samuel was witnessing coup d'état. The divine ruler was being relieved from his duties in favor of a king who would only do bad to them, a king like the other nations. The Lord's response suggests the issue of kingship was symptomatic of a much larger issue, the issue of people's hearts and their trust (or lack thereof) in the Lord God. The Lord's rejection did not start when the elders "gathered together and came to Samuel at Ramah." Rather, many years ago, after the Lord powerfully and majestically delivered his people from slavery, bondage, and death, the people wanted any other king but the Lord. After all, the Lord was concerned about his people's holiness, not their happiness. The people who had been slaves in Egypt, who didn't know freedom and life, wanted to return to a life of servitude and suffering just so their bellies would be full.

From the exodus throughout the rest of the biblical narrative, God's people continually reject him in favor of infinitely lesser, worldly substitutes. This trend of rejecting God for lesser things is evident in every human heart, and it is precisely this trend the ideal king came to remedy. Returning to the biblical narrative, 1 Samuel is where the people reject God's kingship by establishing a king

---

27. Author's translation.

in direct opposition to what he commanded through Moses. This trend away from God continues throughout the existence of the monarchy. God's law is rejected countless times leading to countless troubles. A constant refrain in the lives of the kings is how they failed to follow the way of the Lord. What were the consequences? Both the northern and southern kingdoms were sent into exile. Their feeble attempt to have a kingdom like all the nations does not meet their expectations. Pursuing a kingdom of our own will not satisfy us, either. We were made for another kingdom.

This pattern of rejection runs throughout the monarchy and is brought to light most through the words and actions of the Hebrew prophets. Their words of warning are not heeded and God's people are sent into exile. Even when Israel's physical exile is over and the people are back in the land, they continue to reject God's ideal king. This trend reaches its climax when, during Jesus's trial before Pilate, the issue of Israel's final allegiance comes up. Pilate interrogates the ideal king of Israel while Israel's leaders are there calling for his execution. Pilate, who was no friend to Israel and hoped to spite Israel's leaders, seeks to save Jesus. Israel's leaders claim allegiance to a power, but not God's. "We have no king but Caesar."[28] They choose a power like the other nations. Since we will examine John 18–19 later, we must leave our discussion of Israel's choice before Pilate. However, the elders' choice in John's text is not only similar to the elders in Samuel's day, it is the completion and fulfillment of the rejection begun in 1 Sam 8.

All these details thus far are rich with irony. The elders are demanding a king. But, the Israelites had *the* King since the exodus. Beginning in Egypt, the Lord won victory after victory through the leadership of Moses, Joshua, and the judges. Yet, despite all his work, the people still want a king they can see and hear, a king more like the nations. After a repeated cycle of success, sin, failure of the people, and the subsequent rescue by the Lord, the people believe it is time that the Lord step down from his post and allow man to take over permanently. How tragic. Every leader up to this point has failed, from Moses to Samuel, because no leader yet has

---

28. John 19:15.

The Ideal King

the character and devotion to the Lord necessary to rule the people well. This reality repeats throughout the Old Testament until the ideal king comes.

Most tragic of all was that Samuel's warning went unheeded. Although Samuel obeyed the Lord and gave Israel a king, he also prophesied for the Lord and warned Israel in the strongest way possible where this poorly instituted monarchy would lead.

> He [Samuel] said, "This is what the king who will reign over you will claim as his rights: He will take your sons and make them serve with his chariots and horses, and they will run in front of his chariots. Some he will assign to be commanders of thousands and commanders of fifties, and others to plow his ground and reap his harvest, and still others to make weapons of war and equipment for his chariots. He will take your daughters to be perfumers and cooks and bakers. He will take the best of your fields and vineyards and olive groves and give them to his attendants. He will take a tenth of your grain and of your vintage and give it to his officials and attendants. Your male and female servants and the best of your cattle and donkeys he will take for his own use. He will take a tenth of your flocks, and you yourselves will become his slaves."[29]

Notice how many times the word *take* is used in such quick succession. When items are repeated in the Bible, particularly the Old Testament, understand that the author intends to emphasize the repeated word or idea.[30] Here is a list of things this king will take: sons, daughters, fields, vineyards, olive groves, grain and vintage, male servants, female servants, best of the cattle and livestock, and, when necessary, even his own people as slaves. That's a lot of taking. But, if the purpose is for the good of the nation, maybe this is excusable as a necessary evil? No. The text is clear. This imperial accumulation will be for "*his* chariots," to "plow *his* ground" (which was once "yours"), to "harvest *his* crops" (again, once "yours"), to be perfumers, cooks, and bakers. The fields, vineyards,

---

29. 1 Sam 8:11–17.
30. Alter, *Art of Biblical Narrative*, 181.

olive groves, and livestock will go "to *his* attendants" or "*his* own use" (emphasis added). This is deplorable. Yet, archaeology suggests such imperial accumulation may have been commonplace about the time of the united kingdom, and therefore not foreign to the Israelites.

> The cultural heritage of the important kingdom of Ugarit, which had ceased approximately 130 years before the united monarchy, may well have lived on in those contemporary city kingdoms. Compulsory military conscription, enforced labor for public projects, the duty to provide military equipment, the recruitment of female workers for domestic labor at the royal palace and the confiscation of real estate for the king's use, practices associated with the monarchical system of neighboring peoples by Samuel were current at Ugarit.[31]

A king must take what he does not have to keep what he did not earn. For the Israelite king to be like the other nations, he would do the same.

The elders' choice for a worldly king would lead them down a road they had left only a few generations ago, and then only because the Lord's power was infinitely greater than any imperial regime. In the words of the Lord through Samuel, the Lord said the day would come when Israel would "cry out" for relief from the kings they had chosen.[32] The Hebrew word that translates to "cry out" is loaded with significance since it is the same word and translation as "they cried out," which described the people's desperate plea under the yoke of Egyptian slavery.[33] Through Samuel, the Lord tells his people that, by choosing a king like all the other nations, they are asking for a tyrant, and, by choosing to be like the other nations, they are unwittingly choosing slavery.

Despite this grave warning, the people still affirm their desire for a king, a king like the other nations, a king to fight their

---

31. Arnold and Williamson, *Dictionary of the Old Testament*, 612.
32. 1 Sam 8:18.
33. Exod 2:23.

The Ideal King

battles.[34] Even after Israel had their first king and Samuel chose to step away from leadership, he again reminded them how precarious their situation was. They now had a king, a king who was to be a very particular way and not like the other nations. And, they were to submit themselves to the prescribed king. If they did so, good. But, woe to them if they decided they knew better than God concerning where real power lay. One of Samuel's final words to them must have fallen on deaf ears. Samuel said, "You will realize what an evil thing you did in the eyes of the Lord when you asked for a king."[35] Did they really believe any human king could ever eclipse the power of the God who spoke the sun, moon, and stars into existence? Did they really believe their designs for a king were better than God's perfect design, a design that kept him where he belonged, on the throne? I suggest the answer is yes. I believe we would answer yes too.

When you read carefully the words of Jesus about what he did and what he said, and then you read about how he expects his followers, those who are identifying with his kingdom and affirming his kingship, to live, you read of a king whose ways are diametrically opposed to the world. Yet, we modern Jesus-followers often prefer our ways and means over his own. We wrestle with what Jesus really meant when he spoke of loving our enemies, or when he said how nearly impossible it is for the rich to enter heaven. We are tempted to spiritualize his words so as to make the demands on our own preferred way of life easier. I know this is a constant struggle for me. Admittedly, the Jesus I have created in my own mind, the Jesus that has been preached in modern, imperial, wealthy churches is more comfortable.

David Platt wrote *Radical: Taking Back Your Faith from the American Dream* in 2010 in which he shined the light on the problems with modern, wealthy churches. This book was influential to the larger evangelical world, and it was influential to me. In it, Platt shares a story that fits well with our investigation of the ideal king and the evil desire to be like all the nations:

---

34. 1 Sam 8:20.
35. 1 Sam 12:17.

Really . . . Like the Nations?

I remember when I was preparing to take my first trip to Sudan in 2004. The country was still at war, and the Darfur region in western Sudan had just begun to make headlines. A couple of months before we left, I received a Christian news publication in the mail. The front cover had two headlines side by side. I'm not sure if the editor planned for these particular headlines to be next to each other or if he just missed it in a really bad way.

On the left one headline read, "First Baptist Church celebrates New $23 Million Dollar Building." A lengthy article followed, celebrating the church's expensive new sanctuary. The exquisite marble, intricate design, and beautiful stained glass were all well described in vivid detail.

On the right was a much smaller article. The headline for it read, "Baptist Relief Helps Sudanese Refugees." Knowing I was about to go to Sudan, my attention was drawn. The article described how 350,000 refugees in western Sudan were dying of malnutrition and might not live to the end of the year. It briefly explained their plight and sufferings. The last sentence said the Baptists had sent money to help relieve the suffering of the Sudanese. I was excited until I got to the amount.

Now, remember what was on the left: "First Baptist Church Celebrates New $23 Million Building." The article on the right was, "Baptists have raised $5,000 to send to refugees in western Sudan."

Five thousand dollars.

That is not enough to get a plane into Sudan, much less one drop of water to people who need it.

Twenty-three million dollars for an elaborate sanctuary and five thousand dollars for hundreds of thousands of starving men, women, and children, most of whom were dying apart from faith in Christ.

Where have we gone wrong?

How did we get to the place where this is actually tolerable?[36]

---

36. Platt, *Radical*, 15–16.

The Ideal King

Indeed, where have we gone wrong? We go wrong every time we prefer to do things like the other nations as opposed to the way God has intended it. Whether we like it or not, Jesus's life, words, and ministry are rather simple and clear. Nothing he did was like the nations. Nothing he did was complicated. It's just hard.

I digress. Our journey toward calvary where the ideal king was enthroned must continue through the line of Israelite kings. It is necessary to take brief looks at some of Israel's best and worst kings, all the while remembering this is the type of king the people wanted. There will be kings who are closer to the ideal than others, but even the good kings functioned as a fantastic foil for the ideal king. Our journey, then, begins with Israel's first king, Saul.

Yeah, He Looks Like a King

After the elders of Israel demand a king like all the other nations Samuel goes out to find this new king through the Lord's guidance. The elders get what they ask for in Saul, the son of Kish. This is how the Bible introduces Saul: "There was a Benjamite, a man of standing, whose name was Kish son of Abiel, the son of Zeror, the son of Bekorath, the son of Aphiah of Benjamin. Kish had a son named Saul, as handsome a young man as could be found anywhere in Israel, and he was a head taller than anyone else."[37] Saul was as good looking as any man in all of Israel, and he was bigger than everyone else. Since first impressions are remarkably important, and if you are trying to fit in with all the other like-minded kings, you need to look like an imperial, politically savvy, rich king. Enter Saul.

Saul was installed as king over Israel and reigned for forty-two years, beginning at age thirty.[38] One of Saul's first acts as king was rescuing the city of Jabesh Gilead.[39] I bet here the people must have been rather excited. The king they wanted did the deed they

---

37. 1 Sam 9:1–2.
38. 1 Sam 13:1.
39. 1 Sam 11:1–11.

wanted, defending them from their enemies. But, the honeymoon phase ended.

Two major instances are mentioned in Scripture where Saul chose to do things his way as opposed to the Lord's way. The ideal king was to be only concerned with the Lord's will, not his own. The first instance came when the Lord, through Samuel, gave a command for Saul to wait for a period of time before attacking the Philistines and, only with Samuel, offer a sacrifice. Saul got impatient. He did not want to wait on Samuel. Remember, though, the command to wait originated from God, not Samuel. Saul's impatience was reflective of a deeper issue in his heart, he would not wait on God. Later, Saul was given a command to "totally destroy" the Amalekites. This command included everything the Amalekites owned. Instead of obeying, Saul picked what he wanted to destroy and what he wanted to save.[40] In both instances Saul chose to do what he considered best rather than what God had spoken. Waiting and focusing on God was a boundary marker between Israel's kings and the other nations. Moses said the king was to "learn to revere the Lord his God and follow carefully all the words of this law and these decrees and not consider himself better than his fellow Israelites."[41]

On top of the two specific instances where Saul considered his own way better than God's, he did yet another thing imperial kings were known to do, something Samuel specifically warned the Israelites their future kings would do. Samuel warned the elders the kings would naturally fall into a cycle of taking the best from the people for his own gain. First Samuel 14:52 says, "All the days of Saul there was bitter war with the Philistines, and whenever Saul saw a mighty or brave man, he took him into his service." Simply having a king like the nations to fight battles for Israel did not ultimately solve any problem. Violence never destroys violence, but only perpetuates it. Not only did Israel's king fail to do what they hoped—vanquish their enemy—but he also did what they were told he would do. He took every "mighty or brave man"

---

40. 1 Sam 15.
41. Deut 17:19–20.

The Ideal King

for himself. What would you expect? If you are going to forge an empire of power, political savvy, and wealth you must have the means of protecting it. How do you protect it? Take the best for yourself and create a dependency among the people so as to ensure your longevity. Sound familiar?

Saul's rejection of the ways of the Lord led to his rejection.[42] From his rejection of the Lord and the Lord's subsequent rejection of him, Saul's life began to quickly unravel. Saul's successor was chosen by God, a man after God's own heart. Saul was not too happy about this new royal line. He wanted his own son Jonathan to rule after his passing. Rather than showing humility and understanding that God can do as he wishes with his world and his people, Saul tries to do everything he can to protect his imperial legacy. Just to maintain his own control he tries killing his newly anointed successor.[43] He fails, and his downward spiral is tragic, even killing the Lord's priests.[44] He dies on the battlefield, as does Jonathan. The tragic irony of Saul's story is the reality that the elders of Israel got what they wanted. They found a man in his prime who was physically more impressive than any in Israel. His success in battle early in his reign set a bar he could not continue to meet. His entire reign was spent in war. When he died, Israel was no closer to the end of war than when he began. Suffice it to say Saul was not the ideal king, nor was he a good start toward the ideal king.

So, the monarchy got off to a rough start. First runs at anything are often bumpy. Maybe after working out some kinks, the next king will fare better? Our next king in line after Saul is David, a man after God's own heart.

---

42. 1 Sam 15:26.
43. 1 Sam 18:10–11.
44. 1 Sam 22:6.

Really . . . Like the Nations?

A Man After God's Own Heart

King David is easily one of the most famous characters in the Bible. Familiarity with David seems often based on a relatively few factors. First, David was the one who had Bathsheba. Second, despite his sin with Bathsheba, he was called a man after God's own heart. It seems popular opinion believes David to be the quintessential Israelite king. While he may well be better than most, to say he is *the* ideal king would be a significant mistake. Not only does he stray from Moses's prescription in Deut 17, but when you later compare him to Jesus, his dissimilarities are rather obvious. Let's take a closer look.

Far, far too much ink has been spilled writing about David for me to offer yet another survey of David's life. His status as the youngest of the family and tender of livestock is well known. His being anointed future king of Israel and defeat of Goliath are equally well known. Our Christian tradition also understands David to be a prolific writer of our psalms. These are things children's Bibles would naturally include. There are other truths about David.

One of the most important aspects of David was his proclivity for war. David was in charge of the united kingdoms's great military expansion over which his son Solomon ruled. David was a skilled warrior. The people wrote a little ditty about him, one that infuriated his predecessor. The people danced and sang: "Saul has slain his thousands, David his tens of thousands."[45] This simple rhyme is rather important as it tells of a main feature of David's rule. How does David's ability with a sword align itself with the ideal king?

In Deut 17 the Lord, through Moses, said the ideal king was not to acquire for himself many horses. We learned the acquisition of horses was ultimately a display of military power. The ideal king was not to worry himself with amassing for himself a standing army ready to move at his whim. The ideal king was to concern himself with learning humility and trust in God in all circumstances. This faith would have been (as it is now) a radical departure from the

---

45. 1 Sam 18:7.

militaristic imperial regimes of the ancient Near East. But, that was the point. The Lord delivered his people from Egypt not so they might become the premiere imperial power in the ancient world; rather, the Lord's people were rescued so that they might be his treasured possession, a "kingdom of priests."[46]

King David, though, was a warrior. His journey to the throne included a victory over Goliath.[47] Like Saul, David started well. He went out against a greater foe with superior weapons and faced him with only one advantage. When facing Goliath, David said, "You come against me with sword and spear and javelin, but I come against you in the name of the Lord Almighty, the God of the armies of Israel, whom you have defied."[48] No imperial power or military armament could ever defeat the Lord. Here, David understood that. At this point in his life, he had already defeated a lion and a bear while protecting his father's sheep.[49] David trusted in the God who spoke all things into existence; his trust was honored, and David defeated Goliath. As a result of his victory, David was conscripted into the king's service and fought numerous battles. Saul, who knew David was anointed the future king over Israel, gave his daughter Michal to David in marriage so long as he carried out a particular militaristic feat (hoping, of course, David would die carrying out the mission). First Samuel 18:25 says, "Saul replied, 'Say to David, "The king wants no other price for the bride than a hundred Philistine foreskins, to take revenge on his enemies."' Saul's plan was to have David fall by the hands of the Philistines." Saul is speaking just like an imperial king. What he desires from his enemies in nothing short of simple bloodlust. David does not simply acquiesce to the king's request, but willingly doubles the king's demand and brings back two hundred Philistine foreskins. David was a man of war.

Despite David's liking for combat, he still is called a man after God's heart. His psalms drip with his fear and reverence of

---

46. Exod 19:6.
47. 1 Sam 17.
48. 1 Sam 17:45.
49. 1 Sam 17:36.

the Lord. On two separate occasions, David had a chance to take revenge on Saul, who had tried multiple times to kill him. On both occasions, he let Saul live. David would not dare touch the Lord's king, no matter how far from the truth he had strayed. Yet, with all the positives surrounding David, he still was not Israel's best example of the ideal king.

Imperial kings take from their subjects. One day, when Israel's armies were fighting, David was walking around the palace and saw a woman bathing. Her husband was fighting with Israel's armies on the front. When David saw her he desired her and acquired her. In the course of their affair Bathsheba became pregnant. David had a mess on his hands. He figured the best way to solve it was to bring back Uriah, her husband, get information about the army, get him drunk, send him home, and have him sleep with his wife. Then, it would be easy to say Bathsheba's child was her husband's. But, Uriah was honorable. While his brothers-in-arms were sleeping under the stars, he felt it would dishonor them to go and sleep under his roof with his wife. When David's attempts failed, he sent Uriah back to the army with a letter with specific commands to place Uriah where the fighting was fiercest. Those instructions included withdrawing from the front but leaving Uriah, thereby securing his doom.[50] It's war.

Tragic, is it not? There's an old proverb that says power corrupts. Even amid the better kings of Israel like David, power swayed their hearts far from the Lord's way toward their own way. The power Moses decried as only a tool of the nations and not the tool of the ideal king created opportunities where the gluttony of the human heart, whether food, power, money, women, etc., could be satisfied. And such gluttonous attitudes were antithetical to following God (might I add, such ideas are still antithetical to following God). The ideal king was not to acquire worldly, imperial power, but the power of humility and faith through his daily pursuit of the truth of God.

I hope the portrait of David here does not paint him in a purely imperial light. That's not the case. David did demonstrate

---

50. 1 Sam 11.

humility and love for the Lord's law. The Psalms highlight David's love for God. But the fact remains, David was not the ideal king. There is another textual clue which sheds light on the biblical understanding of David's preference for war.

In 2 Sam 7 David expresses his desire to build for the Lord a "house." David expresses this desire to the Lord's prophet Nathan. The Lord, through Nathan, tells David that not he but his son will be the one to build the Lord's temple. One of the many fascinating aspects to the Old Testament is the various perspectives included throughout its pages. The histories in 1 and 2 Samuel and 1 and 2 Kings are retold from another historical vantage point, after the monarchy failed to do what the elders of Israel hoped. When 1 and 2 Chronicles were written, the kings were a distant memory, and only the hope of the ideal king and the restored Israelite kingdom remained. Reading Samuel and Kings alongside Chronicles shows where the different authors attempted to explain different events from different perspectives. The Lord's denial of David's desire to build a kingdom includes a fascinating perspective. The Chronicler describes a conversation between David and his son Solomon. The text says,

> Then he called for his son Solomon and charged him to build a house for the Lord, the God of Israel. David said to Solomon: "My son, I had it in my heart to build a house for the Name of the Lord my God. But this word of the Lord came to me: 'You have shed much blood and have fought many wars. You are not to build a house for my Name, because you have shed much blood on the earth in my sight. But you will have a son who will be a man of peace and rest, and I will give him rest from all his enemies on every side. His name will be Solomon, and I will grant Israel peace and quiet during his reign. He is the one who will build a house for my Name. He will be my son, and I will be his father. And I will establish the throne of his kingdom over Israel forever.'"[51]

---

51. 1 Chr 22:6–10.

Really... Like the Nations?

Why 2 Samuel did not record this conversation and 1 Chronicles did is a fascinating question. I'm speculating, but it seems that there might be a theological point being made here. The king like the other nations was an outright rejection of the Lord who was the only one actually capable of keeping Israel from experiencing the horrors of exile. Is it possible the writer of Chronicles knew what the ideal king was to be like and how drastically different the kings turned out to be? Even David, one of the better kings, contrasted significantly with the king the Lord prescribed.

The writer of Chronicles mentions the reason why David was denied the opportunity to build the temple. David was a man of blood. The Lord said the many battles and bloodshed in his sight *are the reason* why David was unable to build the temple. How much more clear could the text get about the nature of the ideal king? Furthermore, the reason Solomon was chosen to build the temple was precisely because he was not a man of war, but a man of peace. When David was on his deathbed giving his exhortation to Solomon as he was about to take the kingdom, some of David's exhortations included more bloodshed. One person, Shimei, who called down curses on David, was given a promise by David he would never harm him. Well, it just so happens that when David dies, he will technically have kept his promise, but David told Solomon regarding Shimei: "But now, do not consider him innocent. You are a man of wisdom; you will know what to do to him. Bring his gray head down to the grave in blood."[52] David continues to bloody his hands until (and after) the time of his death. Was David's desire to build the Lord a temple admirable? Yes. David was never condemned for his request. Rather, he was praised for his desire, and his desire was to be fulfilled by his own son. But, he was not the builder because his hands were too bloody. David acquired too many horses.

Christ-followers today honor David, and rightly so. David was called a man after God's own heart. David desired to build the Lord a temple. David wrote many, many psalms that dripped with his own awareness of his sinfulness and need of the Lord. Modern

---

52. 1 Kgs 2:9.

believers often find themselves simply praying David's words as their own since they so well capture the issues of the human heart. But, we cannot turn a blind eye to one of the most important lessons concerning violence, military power, and following the ways of the Lord. The ideal king was not to acquire many horses. In plain language the ideal king was not to be a man of war. Defending the Lord's people is the Lord's job. When we turn to the prophets, one of the prophets records a word from the Lord that almost sounds sarcastic as the Lord mockingly asks where that militaristic defender was when Israel's enemies marched on the capital? Ironically, still today we too often argue our right to defend ourselves as if this world is our only life to live. Look, if my best life is now, I certainly don't want heaven. The Scriptures describe things that are worse than physical death. Do we really believe the full testimony of Scripture?

David's hands were bloody with the blood *of* his enemies. The ideal king, Jesus, had bloody hands too. Only his hands were bloody from his own blood *for* his enemies.

Is it possible the Chronicler knew well the utter joke military power is in solving the real problems of the human condition? The Lord certainly did. That's why through Moses he told Israel's kings not to seek power the way the world does. Worldly power is too fragile. There's always a bigger fish, right? David's bloody hands disqualified him from his greatest spiritual desire. And *the* reason Solomon was preferred against David was his being a man of peace.

Christians, it certainly looks like the Scriptures are clear concerning the ability of those who follow the Lord to use violence. If you are still in doubt, look at Jesus. We'll turn to him shortly, but as *the* ideal king offering *the* way of the kingdom, do you see him ever command the use of violence to his followers? Do any of the apostles use violence? If we follow Jesus, can we be violent?

David, as fine as he was in many ways, was not the ideal king. David displayed great faith in God. At the same time, however, David also showed a gluttonous heart which he often satisfied, whether through women like Bathsheba or war. David's consequences were steep. The son born to him from Bathsheba died within his first week of life. Nor was David allowed to be at the temple because he was a man with bloody hands. The search for the ideal king continues. What about Solomon? At least he was a man of peace.

He Asked for Wisdom!

King Solomon was the third and final king over united Israel. Following his death the kingdom split into a northern and southern kingdom, and those kingdoms faced moral and theological decline until each kingdom was exiled. The monarchy the elders wanted from Samuel turned out quite differently than they had hoped. Then again, maybe they did not realize their hopes were only idealistic, and the logical end of a kingdom secured by such fleeting powers like might, politics, and wealth was exile.

King Solomon was the second son of David and Bathsheba. He is the promised son to rule and eventually build the Lord's temple.[53] While one of Solomon's older brothers, Adonijah, tried setting himself as king when David was quite old, it was Solomon to whom the kingdom was transferred upon David's death.[54] Before dying, David told Solomon, "So be strong, act like a man, and observe what the Lord your God requires: Walk in obedience to him, and keep his decrees and commands, his laws and regulations, as written in the Law of Moses."[55] David's last words include the command to observe what the Lord requires. David may not have had a problem with loving wealth, but he did love women and war. The Lord's ideal king was to be different.

Solomon took his father's advice and sought to follow the Lord. Solomon was by no means perfect, but he began rather well. Traditionally thought to be the author of Proverbs, Solomon is the one who wrote, "The fear of the Lord is the beginning of

---

53. 2 Sam 7.
54. 1 Kgs 1.
55. 1 Kgs 2:2–3.

The Ideal King

knowledge."[56] Such a proverb was not simply a pretty landscape picture with those words hanging inspirationally in his office. Solomon lived out a fear of the Lord, at least a little while. During his good years, the Lord came to Solomon with a mind-blowing offer: "Ask for whatever you want me to give you."[57] Of all things Solomon could have chosen, he asked for wisdom!

If you were brutally honest with yourself, if the Lord came to you with the exact same proposal tonight, what would you ask for? While I am not certain what exactly I'd say, I rather doubt my first thought would be wisdom. This request is indicative of a heart that feared the Lord and one that knew the gravity of the matters ahead of him. Solomon responded, saying, "Now, Lord my God, you have made your servant king in place of my father David. But I am only a little child and do not know how to carry out my duties. Your servant is here among the people you have chosen, a great people, too numerous to count or number. So give your servant a discerning heart to govern your people and to distinguish between right and wrong. For who is able to govern these great people of yours?"[58] What humility! Here is a king who at this point looks a great deal like the ideal king Moses prescribed in Deut 17. Solomon understood his smallness and the Lord's grandeur. Solomon seemingly understood that securing his empire might require a strength far greater than military power, numerous political alliances, or money. Solomon made a wise choice.

Yet, another tragedy is on the horizon. Not all that looks well ends well. In 1 Kgs 3 there is a verse often breezed by on the way to Solomon's fine request. This verse suggests a preference of Solomon's that may well be exacerbated leading to his own downfall. In 1 Kgs 3:1 we learn Solomon made an alliance with Pharaoh of Egypt by marrying his daughter. One foreign wife was never condemned by a king. But, since the Bible simply covered too much history to record every fact of every king, it had to be selective. In the same chapter where Solomon's wisdom is honored, why

---

56. Prov 1:7.
57. 1 Kgs 3:5.
58. 1 Kgs 3:7–9.

include such a small, seemingly innocuous detail about Solomon's treaty with Egypt through marriage? Maybe the author is hoping to keep us from leaping onto Solomon's bandwagon too hastily.

Things go well for Solomon for quite a while. With astonishing insight and wisdom, Solomon judges rightly between two women arguing over a baby both claimed was their own.[59] Solomon's wisdom became world famous.[60] And, eventually, so did his massive building project.

The entirety of Solomon's life is covered in 1 Kgs 1–11. In those short eleven chapters, about a third is devoted to his preparations for the temple, building the temple, and dedicating the temple. Through the course of these events his wisdom remains a significant sub-theme. In his prayer of dedication of the finished temple, Solomon wisely recognizes this temple as merely a symbol of God's presence, not his actual presence. Solomon says, "But will God really dwell on earth? The heavens, even the highest heaven, cannot contain you. How much less this temple I have built!"[61]

Solomon's choice of wisdom was blessed by the Lord. Through his wisdom Solomon became famous, and with that fame came phenomenal wealth. First Kings 10 describes Solomon's splendor in vivid detail. His visitors traveled the globe for an audience with the king. When the people came they did not come alone, but bore the king gifts.[62] Solomon ended up with thousands upon thousands of horses, and more wealth than one could imagine.[63] But, somewhere between these biographical chapters on Solomon, his heart began to stray from the Lord. By the time Solomon died the biblical text seems to suggest he died apart from the Lord. What happened? He failed to uphold the prescribed king's job description.

Moses warned the kings not to acquire horses, wealth, or many wives. Solomon's Achilles heel was women.

---

59. 1 Kgs 3:16–27.
60. 1 Kgs 4:34.
61. 1 Kgs 8:27.
62. 1 Kgs 10:23–25.
63. 1 Kgs 10:23–29.

> King Solomon, however, loved many foreign women besides Pharaoh's daughter—Moabites, Ammonites, Edomites, Sidonians, and Hittites. They were from nations about which the Lord had told the Israelites, "You must not intermarry with them, because they will surely turn your hearts after their gods." Nevertheless, Solomon held fast to them in love. He had seven hundred wives of royal birth and three hundred concubines, and his wives led him astray. As Solomon grew old, his wives turned his heart after other gods, and his heart was not fully devoted to the Lord his God, as the heart of David his father had been. He followed Ashtoreth the goddess of the Sidonians, and Molek the detestable god of the Ammonites. So Solomon did evil in the eyes of the Lord; he did not follow the Lord completely, as David his father had done.[64]

The women he loved "turned his heart after other gods." This chapter concludes Solomon's life and the text never suggests there was a repentant heart in Solomon before his death. We simply don't know. But, what is interesting about Solomon is a second history that runs along his biographical chapters in 1 Kings. Solomon's own literary tradition shows a similar downward trajectory with the introduction of the many women.

Proverbs, Song of Songs, Ecclesiastes, and a number of psalms are attributed to Solomon. But, the three major works are the three books he wrote. If those books are taken in the following order, Proverbs, Song of Songs, and Ecclesiastes, there is an interesting insight gained into Solomon's life not shared in the biographical chapters. Proverbs displays a profound wisdom relying upon God. First Kings 10 mentions Solomon's prolific output of proverbs during his life. Proverbs 31 ends with a chapter on the ideal woman, one which Solomon believes to exist, but apparently never finds himself (maybe because his heart was the issue, and not the women). Ironically, Song of Songs, which Christians today often read as an allegory concerning Christ's love for his church, contains a man's vociferous pursuit of a young woman. Sadly, there's

---

64. 1 Kgs 11:1–6.

no reason to assume this woman is Solomon's first wife. Due to the evidence of his having loved hundreds of women, it may well be his passionate pursuit of this young lady was more of a routine for him. Song of Songs, then, might correspond to Solomon's life as he acquired many women, a sign his wise heart is waning in wisdom. His literary life ends with Ecclesiastes. This book has as a refrain, "This too was meaningless." In the course of Solomon's final work, he decries everything: women, money, power, and even wisdom as meaningless. Even the positive few verses that end the book are likely not written by Solomon himself, but a theological editor later in Israel's history. Like the Chronicler, this editor, too, saw the folly of a life in pursuit of worldly, tangible things when the eternal, unending, glorious God of creation offered himself to his people.

How many people today are ruined by their relational exploits? I work in Christian education, and I don't think I am stretching to truth to say that relationally broken families are not uncommon. These families are broken by pursuit of power, money, and other relationships. The toll is massive, far greater than parents might know. What is heartbreaking about this brokenness is the possibility of preventing it. No, preventing it isn't easy. But, I argue, it is simple. Moses prescribes it in Deut 17. Commit yourself to studying the law of the Lord, see his goodness, and consider yourself no better than your brothers. In other words, learn humility, contentment, and joy as you follow the Lord. This theme is littered throughout the pages of Scripture, and ultimately embodied perfectly in the ideal king, King Jesus.

Up to this point none of the three kings over united Israel fared well. The imperial hopes of the Israelite elders failed. After Solomon's death, the kingdoms split and marched straight toward exile. The Northern Kingdom went into exile in the eighth century BC, followed by the Southern Kingdom in the seventh century BC.

A Tale of Two Kingdoms

The story of the two kingdoms following Solomon's death and subsequent splitting into a northern and southern kingdom is rather

The Ideal King

tragic. Rehoboam was the first king of the Southern Kingdom (Judah) and Jeroboam was king in the Northern Kingdom (Israel).[65] Jeroboam started Israel off by committing idolatry through the institution of cultic high places and installing whomever desired to serve as priests.[66] Jeroboam showed absolute disregard for the Lord's words. Likewise, too, Rehoboam and his kingdom, Judah, started off by idolatry, setting for themselves cultic high places and raising Asherah poles.[67] Judah not only had a king like the other nations, but started following suit in other areas like including male shrine prostitutes as part of the cultic worship.

The tale of two kingdoms comes from two biblical sources being the books of Kings and the books of Chronicles. Walton and Hill write, "The purpose of the books of Kings is to demonstrate that the kings of Israel and Judah failed to live up to the ideals of the kingship covenant and that God was therefore justified in exiling his people."[68] These books recount king after king in quick succession showing how the decline into indecency went unimpeded through generations. Kings and Chronicles prove Samuel's prophecy right. Christopher Wright says, "It was kings who split the nation, kings who infringed the traditional pattern of the land tenure, kings who accelerated the economic forces of oppression and inequality, kings whose pride cost the nations dearly in the game of political alliances and wars, kings who introduced, or did little to prevent, recurring popular apostasy and idolatry."[69]

The author of Kings shows how at the foundation of the political turmoil lay spiritual issues rather than the political realities of their times. The Lord was to be central to the life of Israel, not the nationalism that bred arrogance and self-sufficiency. Walton and Hill summarize the message of the books of Kings, saying, "God's presence is more important than a king's presence, and serving

---

65. 1 Kgs 12.
66. 1 Kgs 13:33–34.
67. 1 Kgs 14:22–24.
68. Walton and Hill, *Old Testament Today*, 194.
69. Wright, *Old Testament Ethics*, 231.

God is more important than political and national status."[70] Israel's desire to be like the nations turned out to be a major reason they were exiled to the other nations.

Even though Israel goes into exile, the voice of the Lord keeps proclaiming the hope that Israel's nation would accomplish its call to be the means of blessing to the nations. The prophets remind Israel of their failures, but also of their future. Their future includes the rightful, ideal king ruling over the nation, and eventually the world. It is to the prophets we must turn next.

---

70. Walton and Hill, *Old Testament Today*, 195.

4

Where Have All the Good Kings Gone?

Who Were the Prophets?

THE PROPHETIC VOICES ARE invaluable to the narrative of the Bible. The prophets are those individuals called by the Lord to deliver specific messages at specific points in Israel's history. These messages were often negative as the prophet proclaimed an accusation the Lord brought against the people. Israel did not behave as a nation that loved beauty, justice, mercy, and truth. They did not live as those made and saved to be the Lord's image and likeness to the world. Instead, the people grew to love their own ways and things. The prophets sought to call them from their rebellion. The prophets did not speak the Lord's accusations simply to beat down the Lord's people. Their messages were infused with the hope of reconciliation, renewal, and restored fellowship with the Lord. In modern rhetoric, the prophets would be likened to faithful preachers, much like the title of Gary Smith's *The Prophets as Preachers*.

In Smith's introduction to the prophets, he succinctly describes the prophets' identity and purpose. While they were prophets who brought God's charges against his people, their work included more than levying accusations. Smith writes, "The prophets were preachers who communicated God's words to transform their audience's thinking and social behavior. They were not primarily concerned with writing a record of a historical period, an eschatological chart of future events, or a systematic presentation of their theology. They were real people attempting to communicate urgent messages to friends and even to some enemies."[1] The prophets of old are similar to the preachers of Jesus's gospel. While preachers seek to make historically relevant statements and communicate well-thought-out theology, the primary goal of the preacher's message is to awaken the slumbering soul to see itself as the Lord sees it. The faithful modern sermon highlights the supreme wisdom of fearing the Lord instead of the pseudo-wisdom of the other nations. Much like today's preachers, the ultimate point of the prophetic message had repentance of sin and reconciliation with the Lord as the central message. Repentance and reconciliation were not merely internal, private matters but often involved, if not demands, outward realizations. Sometimes, a change in the way things were done was essential. For example, the leadership of a nation needed changing.

Smith suggests the prophets called for such social and political changes to demonstrate repentance. Smith writes how the prophets "encouraged people to look at themselves from God's perspective and not conform to the prevailing political perspective of the day because of social pressures."[2] What would God's perspective say about the need for a king like the other nations? Why would Israel need a king to fight their battles, supply their needs, feed their mouths, and maintain their economy when the Lord had done all those things successfully? Would Israel, the Lord's people, need a king like the other nations when no other nation succeeded in establishing an everlasting dynasty? No, Israel needed the True King, and the prophets were sent to Israel to remind them of this truth.

1. Smith, *Prophets as Preachers*, 7.
2. Smith, *Prophets as Preachers*, 7.

The Ideal King

The prophetic voices operated in Israel before, during, and after the united and divided monarchies. It is the prophetic voice that is missed during the so-called intertestamental period. The prophets are those who hear directly from and speak directly for God. What the prophets said about kingship and the ideal king gives context to the historical tragedy of the Israelite experiment with worldly kings. Hosea, speaking for the Lord, will ask sarcastically, "Where is your king, that he may save you?"[3] Hosea seems to be saying, "Man, those good kings that could deliver you from every evil, kings like the other nations, where are they again?" Hosea knew that no king nor any earthly power would last forever. Ironically, the king who could save Israel was rejected long before Hosea's time.

The Lord's kingship was rejected under the prophet Samuel's watch. He denounced their desire as evil. When he was approached by the elders of Israel demanding a king, Samuel made his displeasure known, even warning them of future disaster. Samuel knew the bent of their desire was not for the ideal king; the elders wanted a king like the other nations, one to fight their battles. The elders had their own "ideal" king in mind. Whether the elders realized it or not, they would walk a road back toward slavery. History proved Samuel right. From the outset, the kings, like the other nations, began doing what Samuel said they would do. But remember, Samuel was not the first prophet to speak about Israel's ideal king.

Israel's first prophet, Moses, prescribed—or better, limited—the way the Israelite king was to function. Moses had in view a king who did not consider himself better than his brothers and did not act like the kings of other nations. The other nations were not God's treasured possession, like Israel. The Lord called Israel his own unique nation, a kingdom of priests. Just as the nation was to be different, the Israelite king was to be markedly different. Moses prescribed such a king. Moses's king was allowed to have horses, wives, and wealth, but he was not to hoard them or place his trust in them. His primary task was not the nation's defender, political lobbyist, or chief banker; the ideal king functioned primarily like

---

3. Hos 13:10.

a priest maintaining personal and corporate purity. What Moses prescribed before the monarchy began has yet to materialize. At least, not until Jesus.

This chapter will explore text from two prophets, one major prophet, Isaiah, and one minor prophet, Hosea. This division is not due to cultural or prophetic significance but rather something more practical, like the length of their books. Isaiah is sixty-six chapters, Hosea is fourteen. Our study begins with Isaiah.

A Root from Jesse

Isaiah received his call as a prophet in the year King Uzziah died (c. 742 BC).[4] This was a critical moment in the story of Israel and Judah; the fates of the kingdoms hung in the balance. During the seventh century BC, Assyria would rise as a world power and send Israel to exile. Isaiah's ministry takes place in the midst of such global changes. Not only is Isaiah at a critical time in history, his book also "supplies the template for much of the development of the messianic profile."[5] The coming messianic figure promised in Isaiah, and the future ideal king, is realized in one person, Jesus Christ. The clarity of that revelation is still distant to Isaiah. Still, we who are after the cross and have the privilege of the finished biblical narrative from Genesis onward can see what Isaiah saw through shadows.

One of Isaiah's themes throughout the book is what Hill and Walton call the "future ideal Davidic king," seen most centrally in Isa 2, 9, 11, and the Servant Songs of 42–53. Throughout this book, I contend whether the "Davidic" ideal best captures what Moses prescribed as the perfect king. Yes, David's line would bring about the messianic king. Yes, David was a "man after God's own heart." David's many psalms show his devotion to the Lord's commands. However, we must remember the Chronicler who recorded David's words regarding why the Lord did not let him build the Lord's

---

4. Heschel, *Prophets*, 78.
5. Hill and Walton, *Survey of the Old Testament*, 280.

temple. David was with bloody hands. On his deathbed, he ordered his enemies to be killed, the enemies he promised protection to while he was living. Maybe David was a good king, but he was far from ideal. Isaiah 2 is our first text from the prophets where the ideal king is hinted at.

They Will Train for War No More

Isaiah 2:2 records a prophecy regarding the future of Israel that exclaims hope for a better world. Isaiah says the Lord's mountain, the mount upon which Jerusalem sits, will one day be "highest of the mountains" and "all nations will stream to it." Despite Israel's current separation into a northern and southern kingdom, Israel will one day be united. Furthermore, Isa 2:2 also prophesies that a lack of division between any nation will exist when "the last days" come upon us. Peace will reign supreme. There will be no more demilitarized zones between two hostile countries. There will be no more need for army barracks and air force bases scattered in various places so that a surgical strike can be carried out at any time from anyplace. The nations will be united, and their unity will be evident at the mountain of the Lord. In other words, the Lord will rule all nations and will do so through his ideal king.

As the nations arrive for the banquets and parties, the words on the people's lips will not be those of fear, anxiety, or trouble. Instead, their lips will speak of hope realized and joy experienced. Stories of peace restored and hostilities ended will resound throughout the halls of the Lord's temple. Rather than contingency plans being made should political talks go sour, the chatter among the people will be about holiness. Isaiah records the words of the people when they will say, "He will teach us his ways, so that we may walk in his paths."[6] One day, people will finally realize their worldly methods pale in comparison to the way the Lord intended it to be. The Lord has lessons to teach that are not mere propositions but means to true life. The ways of the Lord are those ways

---

6. Isa 2:3.

that are not merely memorized but walked with. The Lord's ways are not burdensome but freeing. The Lord's ways are for life and life abundantly. Isaiah sees a time when all the nations will go to the Lord. In his commentary on Isaiah, Oswalt writes,

> Thus, the going is for the purpose of being taught, and the being taught is for the purpose of walking. There is a profound truth here. Those who will not leave their own self-sufficiency and come to God cannot learn his (and their own) ways. But learning is for the purpose of living. It is not an end in itself (2 Tim. 3:7). Here is one more way in which the scriptural picture of the interlocked partnership of divine and human is displayed. Unless God teaches we cannot walk, but unless we come he cannot teach.[7]

The people will go to the Lord, learn his ways, and then carry his ways out in their rule of the universe. The earliest chapters of Genesis demonstrate rather clearly the purpose of humanity was to rule the earth in the likeness and image of the Lord's rule of the cosmos. When Israel was rescued from Egypt, they were not rescued only because they needed rescue. They were saved for living, learning, and ruling in the likeness and image of God. And, what kind of power is that again?

The ways of the Lord do not refer to amassing a better military, securing more political allies, or stockpiling more cash. Instead, the way of the Lord is faith in the Lord, his abilities, and his wisdom. When Israel was hungry in the desert, the Lord fed them. When they were thirsty, he gave them a drink. When their enemies pursued them, he delivered them. Whenever the Lord's people were in need, and they trusted the Lord to provide and not themselves, the Lord delivered. The writer of Hebrews describes faith like this: "Now faith is confidence in what we hope for and assurance about what we do not see. This is what the ancients were commended for."[8] When the ideal king appears, he will lead his people in a lifestyle where it is evident the Lord's ways are best

---

7. Oswalt, *Book of Isaiah*, 117.
8. Heb 11:1–2.

even when it does not appear to be so. And, in every circumstance where faith in the Lord is displayed, the ideal king will be rewarded and shown to be right. Even death will be welcomed, knowing the Lord has power over death. And, when the ideal king walks out from the grave victorious, the final exclamation point on whether faith actually works will be printed.

In the life of faith, the Lord requires even what seems farfetched to be accepted as fact. The ideal king of Israel was to concern himself principally with the law of the Lord, even writing for himself his own copy. This copy came through laborious copying, not a fancy printer. Personal copies of the Lord's laws simply did not exist. But, for the king, they were the lifeblood of the nation. The ideal king was to so immerse himself in the Law that one day the "law will go out from Zion" and it will go to the nations.[9] The human preference for strong defenses, alliances, and bank accounts will give way to the Lord's preference for righteousness, holiness, peace, and love. What would be the result of such a radical preference? No more war.

Isaiah's prophecy says when the ideal kingdom arrives, "they will beat their swords into plowshares and their spears into pruning hooks. Nation will not take up sword against nation, nor will they train for war anymore."[10] Heschel, in his classic work *The Prophets*, writes that, in Isaiah's time, "the sword is the pride of man; arsenals, forts, and chariots lend supremacy to nations. War is the climax of human ingenuity, the object of supreme efforts: men slaughtering each other, cities battered into ruins. What is left behind is agony, death, and desolation."[11] Since Isaiah's time, not much has changed by way of man's proclivity for war. Modern nations still pride themselves on their military strength as proof of raw power. Countless billions are spent on bettering our methods of being more destructive than other nations, and more terrifying to potential adversaries. For example, the United States spends more on its military power of preservation or adversarial

---

9. Isa 2:3.
10. Isa 2:4.
11. Heschel, *Prophets*, 234.

annihilation than the following seven countries combined. Countless questions arise when such disproportionate spending occurs. Still, the most basic question is whether such power guarantees the safety man so longs for? Is the real problem not embedded in our human hearts?

The one significant change from Isaiah's time is the type of weaponry used. The sword is no longer the pride of man. We are far more sophisticated in our means of killing today. In the days of Isaiah, Israel, and Judah, to take a man's life meant having to look into his eyes. Today, death comes from a distance. Killing can be done impersonally through grenades tossed from yards away, bombs dropped from miles above, or long-range missiles launched from other sides of a continent. Even the modern soldier is armed with weapons that mechanically throw hundreds of bullets in the direction of living persons. No one could argue war is what humans ought to do.

No more war seems inconceivable, right? In our world, it does. But does that make war right? Should the world we all long for be forsaken because of the way the world just is? How will we live as believers in the Lord and his ideal king, Jesus? What is our posture toward the use of force? One day, war will be no more. If that is true, how comfortable are we really praying "Your kingdom come, your will be done" if we know no war is his will?

The Lord, through Isaiah, proclaims a reality humanity longs for, no war. Heschel writes, "What to us seems inconceivable, to Isaiah was a certainty: War will be abolished. They shall not learn war anymore because they shall seek knowledge of the word of God. Passion for war will be subdued by a greater passion: the passion to discover God's ways."[12] Isaiah was confident because of his faith in the Unseen. Isaiah's faith is the faith to which all followers of the Lord are called to emulate. Isaiah saw a time when the way all the nations acted toward one another would be shown for its foolishness. Imperial power was not without problems; no imperial power survived throughout the ages. Why? Every imperial power followed the pattern of the empires it followed, patterns

12. Heschel, *Prophets*, 235.

of violence, politics, and wealth hoarding. Yet, a power far greater exists. This power unattainable by imperial means, power that lasts through the ages and is not subject to decay like weapons, allies, and money, is holiness in the Lord's likeness and image[13] and faith in the Lord's incredible power.[14] Faith and holiness were to be the ideal king's modus operandi.

Isaiah's vision is more practical than first imagined. Isaiah's future vision should not be understood as something merely heavenly. Who would ever live such a life in our world, though? Indeed, such a radical faith in the Lord that all he does is right is overly spiritual. In a matter of a few centuries, Isaiah's words are embodied in the ideal king, Jesus. Where Isaiah hoped that, one day, passion for God's word would trump passion for man's own security through military might, Jesus proclaimed seeking first God's kingdom and all else man needs would come.[15] Maybe Isaiah's vision was not so impractical. Its embodiment in Jesus worked, but his own submission even to violence without responding in kind disarmed violence and death like no army could.

Isaiah 9—A Child Is Born

Every year during Advent, churches turn to Isaiah's prophecy in chapter 9, which speaks of a child being born. This child is no ordinary child, evident in his name. Boys and girls are born and named John, Joe, Suzie, Eric, Samantha, etc. But not this child. Isaiah 9:6 says this child "will be called Wonderful Counselor, Mighty God, Everlasting Father, Prince of Peace." The hope of the world will one day be swaddled in cloths in a stable with his parents. This same child would one day grow up and finally fulfill the expectations of the ideal king. The result would be for the betterment of the entire cosmos.

13. Lev 11:44.
14. Isa 44:24.
15. Matt 6:33.

Where Have All the Good Kings Gone?

Isaiah speaks of the child given to Israel upon whose shoulders the government will be placed.[16] So, already, we see central to Isaiah's vision of Israel's future is a government, a pattern of rule. From the first pages of Genesis, the Lord establishes order and rule in a world bent toward chaos and individual anarchy. Over every sphere of the cosmos, God established kingdoms of space, land, and water. Over those kingdoms were placed kings like the sun and stars, animals, and fish, respectively. But, the chief ruler, the one to rule the entire world after the likeness and image of God, was mankind. We botched it because we followed the wisdom like the other nations, but the Lord did not give up on his design. Man's wisdom is not the only way in the cosmos. Now, Isaiah speaks of the child who will return the universe to order by administering justice according to the wisdom of the Lord. After all, one of his titles will be Wonderful Counselor. This ideal king would "give wondrous counsel, unfailing in the depth of its wisdom. For it is true wisdom which knows that in weakness is strength, in surrender is victory, and in death is life. . . . So this counselor is a wonder because his counsel goes beyond the merely human."[17] Only a king whose primary mission was not the defense of the nation or the accumulation of political allies or wealth but who focused singularly on the law of the Lord and his own personal holiness could rule like the Lord. Moses described that king exactly.[18]

The kings Isaiah was familiar with did not see in death there was life, or in surrender, there was a victory. Moses completely surrendered to the Lord's will during the Israelites' struggles with Egypt. What happened? The Lord split the sea. Israel's kings failed to yield to the Lord in the same fashion until a king came who left his royal position to walk among the lowest of his people. That king eventually gave his life to his people so that they might live.

This future king would be more than a Wonderful Counselor. When this son reigns according to the way the Lord prescribed through Moses, his government will increase without end, and

---

16. Isa 9:6.
17. Oswalt, *Book of Isaiah*, 247.
18. Deut 17:14–20.

The Ideal King

peace will extend into time immemorial.[19] Notice how the rule will increase incrementally along with peace. This ideal king's title will be Prince of Peace. Oswalt writes, "What sort of king is this? He is a peaceful king, one who comes in peace and establishes peace, not by a brutal squashing of all defiance, but through a transparent vulnerability which makes defiance pointless."[20] The king's demeanor will be such that not only will there be no rebellion, but no one will want to rebel. Yet, the kings who have appeared throughout history have faced rebellions. Why? Because the kings of human history preferred some subjects over others. Maybe they were overly brutal or aggressive. Perhaps they were poor, selfish politicians. Perhaps they were motivated only by personal wealth. Whatever the reasons, people became dissatisfied and chose to take up arms. But, this will not happen against Isaiah's ideal king. This king's yoke will be easy and his burden light. The old ways will die. War will be no more. Isaiah comments that "every warrior's boot used in battle and every garment rolled in blood will be destined for burning, will be fuel for fire."[21] The world will finally be as the Lord intended it.

Isaiah sees a time when the world will not simply be how it was intended but be and remain as it ought to be. When the ideal king comes, "he will reign on David's throne and over his kingdom, establishing and upholding with justice and righteousness from that time on and forever."[22] King David was promised an heir who would come to reign on his throne forever.[23] When David ruled over Israel he waged many wars and through the strength of sword expanded the kingdom of Israel. This future ideal king will reign over David's kingdom from David's throne, but he will not reign the way David did. The future king will be radically different socially and behaviorally because he will be uniquely filled with the Lord's spirit. On the contrary, the kingdom will be established,

19. Isa 9:7.
20. Oswalt, *Book of Isaiah*, 248.
21. Isa 9:5.
22. Isa 9:7.
23. 2 Sam 7:13.

expanded, and upheld through justice and righteousness.[24] This king's realm will remain forever because its stability is not built on the sandy foundations of military power, political safety, or economic security. His kingdom is created and stays because of the solid rock of truth, justice, and righteousness after the image and likeness of the Lord of heaven and earth. Psalms 89:14 says, "Righteousness and justice are the foundation of your throne." So shall his throne rule be forever.

What other king of Israel or Judah could be described by saying their personal lives and their political rule were founded in righteousness and justice? None of them. None of the kings of Israel and Judah upheld the expectations of the Lord, Moses included. External pressures caused every individual to crack. Their faith failed at critical junctures in their lives. Moses, who had just witnessed the walls of water on his right and left at the behest of the Lord, chose not to speak to a rock and call forth water, despite the Lord promising fulfillment.[25] Saul preferred his own timing as opposed to the Lord's timing, showing deep down he believed his own ways were preferable to the Lord's.[26] Despite having everything a man could ask for, David so desired another man's wife that he took first her and then her husband's life from him.[27] Solomon loved many, many foreign women. These women not only worshipped false gods but caused Solomon to forsake his own fear of the Lord and bow down to statues of wood and stone.[28] Moses had a crisis of faith; Saul a lust for his own power; David a lust of his eyes caused by his power; Solomon a lust for women not wholly unlike his father except in quantity. I could continue through the list of kings, but the point would only be belabored.

While not completely terrible, and many have some bright spots, these kings only highlighted the need for a king to faithfully follow the precepts laid down by the Lord through Moses. In

24. Isa 9:7.
25. Num 20:8–12.
26. 1 Sam 13:1–13.
27. 2 Sam 11.
28. 1 Kgs 11:1–5.

Isaiah, the promise of that king has not been forgotten. The Lord will succeed in bringing about what he said he would do. The ideal king would one day come, a king whose sole focus was justice and righteousness and whose faith would never waver, even through torture and death.

Jesse's Root

Isaiah 11 prophesies further about the king who will come from Jesse's line and establish a kingdom like none other. This future ruler of Israel will not rule over Israel's borders only; rather, his rule will be cosmic in scope. There will be no part of the created order unaffected by his rule in the likeness and image of God. This king's rule will be such that enemies in nature, like the lion and lamb, will no longer harm one another. Isaiah 11: 6–7 says, "The wolf will live with the lamb, the leopard will lie down with the goat, the calf and the lion and the yearling together; and a little child will lead them. The cow will feed with the bear, their young will lie down together, and the lion will eat straw like the ox." The animal world, red in tooth and claw, will no longer kill or harm because of the king reigning from Jerusalem's throne. The human population, too, will not harm or destroy. The days of death and destruction will end; instead, the earth will be covered with the knowledge of the Lord.[29] Order will rise from the ashes of chaos; harmony will ensue and remain.

To bring about such a kingdom will require a ruler the likes of which the world has never known. Kings, like the other nations, have consistently shown their capacity for chaos because these kings followed the chaos within their own hearts. Kings show themselves as lovers of violence and money, hurting those they are supposed to protect. A king's subjects should flourish. But, as Samuel stated long ago, kings like the other nations take from their people everything for their own royal means.

---

29. Isa 11:9.

Isaiah 11:2 describes the character of this future ruler, saying, "The Spirit of the Lord will rest on him—the Spirit of wisdom and of understanding, the Spirit of counsel and of might, the Spirit of the knowledge and fear of the Lord—and he will delight in the fear of the Lord." This king will be wise and understanding, grounded in the knowledge and fear of the Lord. This type of king is what Israel and Judah lacked. Though there were relatively good kings scattered throughout Israel's history, the majority of the kings were foolish; they trusted in worldly means. Psalms 20:7 says, "Some trust in chariots and some in horses, but we trust in the name of the Lord our God." Many of Israel's kings trusted in chariots and horses, or maybe in Assyrian or Egyptian protection. But trusting and fearing the Lord should be the operating principle of the Lord's people. Moses's original prescription said the ideal king would write his own copy of the law so that "he may learn to revere the Lord his God and follow carefully all the words of this law and these decrees."[30] Fearing the Lord is not simply something you do, as if outward actions themselves could cultivate fear of the Lord. Instead, fearing the Lord is a posture of the heart, a characteristic of a soul profoundly aware of the Lord's beauty and supremacy.

This king, whose heart is bent toward holiness, beauty, and justice, will rule with those ends in mind. Isaiah says this future king will judge with righteousness, not what he sees with his eyes or hears with his ears, but according to what he knows is true.[31] When Isaiah mentions this king "striking the earth," we must be careful to read what Isaiah says the king will strike. He will not come in vengeance with hot weapons and sharp swords. The weapon with which he will strike the earth is the "rod of his mouth" and the "breath of his lips."[32] The weapon here is this king's all-powerful word.

This study seeks to read the Bible not as individual pieces but as a collective whole. Better yet, the Bible is a narrative. Early portions of the story, allusions, and foreshadows, are only understood

30. Deut 17:19.
31. Isa 11:3–4.
32. Isa 11:4–5.

The Ideal King

when their fulfillment is realized. So, when the Bible talks about the "word" as a weapon, the entire narrative sheds light on what Isaiah means by using such imagery for the power of words. In the earliest chapters of the biblical drama, only through the power of the spoken word does the entire universe leap into existence. Stars are born because God spoke to them. Man, formed from the dust, becomes a living creature when the Lord breathes life into his nostrils. Words are powerful. Throughout the biblical narrative, verses speak of the tongue's power. Proverbs 18:21 says, "The tongue has the power of life and death." Jesus describes his ministry as a sword dividing families, father against son, mother against daughter.[33] Since Jesus never literally carries a sword, it is evident that the sword he is referring to is the message of his kingdom and its other-worldly expectations. The writer of Hebrews shows us how the word of God is a living and active sword.[34] Where a literal sword can cut flesh and bone, the sword of the Lord's word can cut between soul and spirit. Finally, in John's Revelation, King Jesus's weapon to silence all his enemies and finally finish death and destruction is not a literal sword, but a sword from his mouth.[35] Since the mouth is an odd place to keep such a sharp object, the logical conclusion in Revelation is John's use of *sword* is a reference to a weapon far more powerful than steel and iron. Jesus simply needs to speak.

The rod of the future king's mouth is none other than his true, holy word. Commenting on Isa 11:5, Oswalt writes, "*He will strike the earth with the rod of his mouth* expresses the moral force possessed by a leader who owes allegiance to no earthly pressure groups. He can say what needs to be said in a given circumstance and the force of the truth is undeniable. The word itself becomes his weapon."[36] The ideal king will abandon his own ways and means to abandon himself to the Lord and his truth. In the future, Jesus will say to Pilate, "In fact, the reason I was born and came

33. Matt 10:34.
34. Heb 4:12.
35. Rev 19:15.
36. Oswalt, *Book of Isaiah*, 281.

into the world is to testify to the truth."[37] The only allegiance this ideal future king has is to the Lord's kingdom, a kingdom built on the foundation of righteousness and justice.[38]

What Isaiah is prophesying sounds incredible because the current experience for Isaiah and his contemporaries differs from this ideal king. Modern followers can't understand how this could be so. I am only guessing here, but I bet many people who claim to follow Christ struggle to believe (and therefore act upon) the truth that evil, death, disease, and decay have been defeated. I wonder if our actions, worldliness, wealth accumulation, and preference for worldly solutions to our problems exist because we are not sure about Jesus's whole gospel. Maybe too good to be true?

Similarly, Isaiah's contemporaries hear about a coming ruler from David's promised line who embodies wisdom and insight because he uniquely will lead the people in obedience to God's will in word and deed. This Israelite king would do more than simply bring peace to the nation; he would bring it to the entire cosmos. Like the Lord, he speaks to the disorder and chaos of life and brings about order, unity, and shalom.

Isaiah: A Summary

Three chapters of Isaiah received detailed attention. However, Isaiah has far more to say about the ideal king and the effects of his rule than this small part. Isaiah condemns Israel's desire to ally itself with pagan nations in Isa 30:1–3. Without seeking the Lord's will, the Lord's people carried out plans the Lord did not make and formed an alliance against the Lord's will, "heaping sin on sin."[39] The Lord's people still believed their greatest allies were imperial powers not dissimilar from the nations they needed protection from. Why not turn to the Lord? Why not seek the God of all creation's defense, the one who splits the seas and calls nebulae

---

37. John 18:37.
38. Ps 89:14.
39. Isa 30:1.

The Ideal King

into existence? Just like in the days of Samuel when Israel first demanded a king, in Isaiah's time the people do things like all the nations. What was the result of their adulterous alliance? The Lord said, "Pharaoh's protection will be to your shame; Egypt's shade will bring you disgrace."[40]

Isaiah prophesies the Lord's words concerning those who make alliances with power other than his. In Isa 31:1–3, the Lord says,

> Woe to those who go down to Egypt for help, who rely on horses, who trust in the multitude of their chariots and in the great strength of their horsemen, but do not look to the Holy One of Israel, or seek help from the Lord. Yet he too is wise and can bring disaster; he does not take back his words. He will rise up against that wicked nation, against those who help evildoers. But the Egyptians are mere mortals and not God; their horses are flesh and not spirit. When the Lord stretches out his hand, those who help will stumble, those who are helped will fall; all will perish together.

People prefer trusting in things their physical eyes can see and their hands can touch. Yet the Lord, through Isaiah, continually calls his people to see not with their limited physical eyes but the eyes that realize reality is more than what meets the eye. St. Paul will later say the believer's greatest battle is not against flesh and blood but the principalities, powers, and the prince of darkness.[41]

Consider the truth of the Bible's call to see the reality behind what we see. For example, consider the Islamic extremist group ISIS. If the nations of the world physically removed the threat of ISIS, would ISIS be eliminated forever? Not necessarily. Why? ISIS is the physical manifestation of an ideological reality. To wage war against an ideological enemy with physical means may slow the ideology's progress, but it will never defeat it. The greatest battlefield of the world is not fought in the physical arena, the one the

---

40. Isa 30:3.
41. Eph 6:12.

eyes see. Instead, our greatest battles are in areas where eyes cannot see, only the true eyes of the heart.

Isaiah prophesies a time when paradise lost will become paradise regained. He describes what will happen when God comes to save, redeem, and rule his people. When that time comes, "the eyes of the blind will be opened, and the ears of the deaf unstopped."[42] Centuries later, the promised king comes and inaugurates the Lord's kingdom by doing the things Isaiah said he would. This ideal king opens blind eyes and deaf ears. The true king shows his power by healing diseases, touching lepers, and raising the dead. And through his death and resurrection, he opens a road called the Holy Way, which will take travelers to the kingdom's capital city with songs of joy.[43]

Hosea: Where Is That King of Yours?

Like Isaiah, Hosea also prophesied to the Northern Kingdom before its exile to Assyria in 722 BC. In the years leading up to Assyria's expansion into Israel, Israel's monarchy was in shambles. Heschel writes, "For Hosea, there was no legitimate king in the country at all. Kingship derived its prerogatives from a divine election; but of the kings who emerged from violence and rebellion, the word proclaims: *They made kings, but not through Me, they shut up princes, but without My knowledge.*"[44]

Hosea's claim against Israel is reminiscent of the closing chapters of Judges: "In those days Israel had no king; everyone did as they saw fit."[45] Rather than the nation relying on God to provide their protection and prosperity, Israel sought the favor of whichever political entity held most power at the moment, whether Egypt or Assyria. Sadly, neither Egypt nor Assyria were allies, neither nation wanted to create the conditions of a flourishing Israelite

---

42. Isa 35:5.
43. Isa 35:8–10.
44. Heschel, *Prophets*, 50.
45. Judg 21:25.

nation. On the contrary, Egypt held Israel captive for centuries. Israel's deliverance *from* Egypt is *the* defining event of the Old Testament. Yet, the people are willing to return to Egypt? Hosea 7:11 says that Israel (or Ephraim in this verse) is "like a dove, easily deceived and senseless—now calling to Egypt, now turning to Assyria." Returning to Egypt is folly, but so is turning to Assyria. Heschel, quoting the words of another scholar, writes, "Assyria has been characterized as the nest of the bird of prey whence 'set forth the most terrible expeditions which ever flooded the world with blood. Ashur was its god, plunder its morality, cruelty and terror its means. No people was ever more abject than those of Ashur; no sovereigns were ever more despotic, more covetous, more vindictive, more pitiless, more proud of their crimes. Assyria sums up within herself all the vices. Aside from bravery, she offers not a single virtue.'"[46] What does it say about the hearts of the people when they seek solace and safety in such an empire?

Hosea foresees Israel's destruction. While there are many secondary causes involved in Israel's destruction, the primary cause is Israel's idolatry and faithlessness. Part of Israel's idolatry and faithlessness is evident in Israel's obsession to have a king like the nations. Israel was called to be of another world, not like these nations. Hosea 13:9-11 says,

> You are destroyed, Israel, because you are against me, against your helper. Where is your king, that he may save you? Where are your rulers in all your towns, of whom you said, "give me a king and princes"? So in my anger I gave you a king, and in my wrath I took him away.

"Where is your king, that he may save you?" What a question! Let us not forget that, in 1 Sam 8, the people demanded from Samuel a king like the other nations. Among the reasons the people gave for this demand was that the king would "lead us and . . . go out before us and fight our battles."[47] Samuel called this desire evil. The Lord would fight Israel's battles if they put their trust in him.

---

46. De Morgan, quoted by A. T. Olmstead, in Heschel, *Prophets*, 49.
47. 1 Sam 8:20.

The ideal king would not be a man of war, but a man of truth. Israel wanted a man of war. Now, Hosea is asking Israel where their man of war is? Where is that king who would be Israel's salvation? Why is Israel on the brink of destruction? Israel's predicament is due to their preference for a king like the other nations rather than God.

Israel's desire for a king was not the issue; the issue was the *kind* of king Israel demanded. Deuteronomy 17 prescribed the ideal king unlike the nations, yet Israel demanded a king like the other nations. What does living like the world get you? What happens when our hopes for protection and prosperity are rooted in those things that grow and wither like the grass? The Israelites in 1 Sam 8 demanded a king on their own terms in hopes that they might gain their happiness on their own terms. Trying to find happiness on your own terms is hopeless. "And out of that hopeless attempt has come nearly all that we call human history—money, poverty, ambition, war, prostitution, classes, empires, slavery—the long terrible story of man trying to find something other than God which will make him happy."[48]

Hosea's message included more than doom. Hosea invited Israel to repent, and should they repent, they would find healing. Hosea 14:4-7 says,

> I will heal their waywardness and love them freely, for my anger has turned away from them. I will be like the dew to Israel; he will blossom like a lily. Like a cedar of Lebanon he will send down his roots; his young shoots will grow. His splendor will be like an olive tree, his fragrance like a cedar of Lebanon. People will dwell again in his shade; they will flourish like the grain, they will blossom like the vine—Israel's fame will be like the wine of Lebanon.

The invitation to repentance is an invitation to restoration. Idolatry and faithlessness is a choice. Likewise, repentance is a choice. Should Israel choose repentance, she will receive life. Should you and I choose repentance, we will receive life. To continue in our idolatry and faithlessness is to attempt to find happiness in

---

48. Lewis, *Mere Christianity*, 49.

The Ideal King

something other than God, which simply does not exist. Israel remains steadfast in her reliance upon powers of this world. As such, Israel fails in her mission. But, God is not done with Israel. In one Man, God raises up a new Israel who chooses properly and a new Moses who leads successfully. This man will also be the ideal king who rules faithfully. This man is Jesus.

5

The Ideal King

Entering The New Testament World

THE PREVIOUS CHAPTERS HAVE presented the biblical picture of the Lord's ideal king from the earliest pages of the scriptural witness through the Old Testament prophets. Time and time again, the Lord's ideal king is juxtaposed with his people's desire for a king like the other nations. The this-worldly kings the people desire are a perpetual disappointment. The people hope for kings to rule and protect them and to create structures for flourishing. The kings fail to satisfy the people's hopes. The people's experience under the kings they so strongly desire is tumultuous at best. Even the best kings cause great harm for their people. For example, while David may have established a strong nation through his military prowess, at the end of his life a feud for the throne begins causing strife in the nation. This strife ultimately leads to a division where the once-united nation splits into two kingdoms, Israel in the north, and Judah in the south. Within a few centuries after the split, the nation of Israel is exiled to Assyria.

The prophets rebuke Israel for their idolatry. The Lord's people are called to recognize their plight is self-inflicted. Yet, amid

The Ideal King

the accusations, the prophets carry a message of hope. One day the king the Lord prescribed through Moses will rule on the throne promised to David. This king will not simply reunite Israel but reunite the cosmos. The future king, who looks nothing like the other nations, will not be a man who relies on military or political power to coerce his subjects. Instead, this king's life, wisdom, love, grace, and humility will demonstrate his true power. He will finally demonstrate the power of light over darkness, the real power of love over the pseudo-power of fear.

What the prophets proclaimed arrives most strangely in the early chapters of the New Testament. To a virgin girl, a boy is born who is destined to rule the nations.[1] The long-awaited king in the Lord's likeness and image arrives without typical royal fanfare. The King of all kings is not welcomed into a royal palace but a drafty stable. Though heralds announced the birth of the Lord's king, the announcement was not made to the wealthy or powerful but to those of low social standing, shepherds.[2] This king was not born in the cultural or economic hub of Israel, but in a small town miles from Israel's capital. His birth sets this king apart from his this-worldly counterparts. As we will see, his entire life, including his birth, death, and resurrection, are all diametrically opposed to the kingdoms and kings of this world.

When the ideal king is born, one major cultural trend has remained consistent throughout Israel's history. Since at least the time of Samuel, the Lord's people have favored the political and military powers of the world over the designs of the Lord's prescriptions. Samuel noted clearly the people's demand for a king was wicked.[3] The people never learned their lesson. Apparently, not even exile changed their minds.

---

1. Matt 1:18–25; Luke 2:1–7.
2. Luke 2:8–20.
3. 1 Sam 8:1–9.

The Ideal King

The King the People Wanted vs. the King the People Needed

After surveying the trajectory of kingship in the Old Testament, our attention now turns to the pages of the New Testament. What we will find in these pages are two competing ideologies of kingship. On the one hand, some Israelites desired a militaristic, worldly king, much like the other nations. A king such as this would be capable of driving out Israel's imperial overlords, the Romans. The hoped-for king would follow in the trajectory of King David or Judas Maccabeus. This was the majority opinion. New Testament scholarship shares the same understanding of first-century Palestine. N. T. Wright's research on first-century Judaism offers supple evidence of Israel's messianic hope. For example, while Wright comments how "no single unified concept of the Messiah" existed in the first century for certain, "messiahs were supposed to fight Israel's great battle against the old enemy and rebuild the Temple as the place where God would meet with his people in grace and forgiveness."[4] Wright lists several instances in Israel's history that serve as examples. In the Old Testament, there was David. Other examples come from the intertestamental period through the mid-second century (c. 400 BC–150 AD). Wright summarizes this period with a quick outline: "Judas Maccabeus defeated the Syrians and cleansed the temple. Herod defeated the Parthians and rebuilt the Temple. Bar-Kochba, the last would-be Messiah of the period, aimed to defeat the Romans and rebuild the Temple."[5]

In Wright's first volume of his seminal series Christian Origins and the Question of God, he describes Israel's history, political structure, and belief system at the time of Jesus's birth. Wright also provides a history of Israel's messianic expectations from the end of the Old Testament to the epoch of Christ. He offers this summary of the messiah's main task as evidenced in the extant material:

---

4. Wright, *Challenge of Jesus*, 85.
5. Wright, *Challenge of Jesus*, 75.

> The main task of the Messiah, over and over again, is the liberation of Israel and her reinstatement as the true people of the creator God. This will often involve military action, which can be seen in terms of judgment as in a law court. It will also involve action in relation to the Jerusalem Temple, which must be cleansed and/or restored and/or rebuilt.[6]

Jesus's ministry and mission accomplished these messianic tasks. Jesus conquered Israel's greatest enemy, Satan.[7] He cleansed God's temple, and then claimed that something greater than the temple is here.[8] Though not necessarily militaristically, Jesus was a warrior. His method of warfare was not with tangible elements like steel and bronze, nor were his ultimate enemies those of flesh and blood. Jesus waged war not against "flesh and blood, but against the rulers, against the authorities, against the powers of this dark world and against the spiritual forces of evil in the heavenly realms."[9] His weapons were far more potent than bronze and steel. His weapon was the truth, and "everyone on the side of truth listens to me."[10]

Jesus waged war against Israel's enemies, enemies within and without ethnic Israel, by exposing the identity of Israel's real enemies. The enemies of God's people were not a particular ethnic group, such as the Romans, but rather people who aligned themselves with the ways of the world over the ways of the Lord. Jesus's warfare was waged against the cosmic forces behind the evil in creation. Jesus cast out demons, healed diseases, and raised the dead. No steel sword, bronze spear, or modern gun can do likewise.[11] The weapons of the world only bring chaos and death. Only the true king, the king with healing in his hands, the king whose power extends beyond geographical borders and into all creation,

6. Wright, *New Testament and the People of God*, 320.
7. John 12:31.
8. Matt 12:6; John 2:13–25.
9. Eph 6:12.
10. John 18:37.
11. Luke 4:18–19; see also, Matt 8–9.

can bring order from chaos. This is what Jesus did. This is what the true messiah, the ideal king, was to do.

But, in Jesus's time, who was looking for such a messiah? Really, only a handful. And, even those who were seeking for the true messiah were surprised when the Messiah found them. Jesus believed the messiah, the king the people needed, was different from the king the people wanted. Prophets before Jesus, like Moses, Samuel, and Isaiah, also knew the people needed someone different than what they wanted. The ideal king would not wage war as the world does through military power, politics, or money; instead, this king would wage war with truth, which is infinitely more powerful than any human concoction of pseudo-power. The ideal king would combat the world's evil through faith, hope, grace, forgiveness, and self-sacrificial love.

No King but Caesar

During Jesus's trial before Pilate, Israel's religious and social leaders show their true political allegiance. Jesus has been questioned by Pilate, and Pilate desires to free him. John 19:12–16 records the following exchange between Pilate and Israel's leaders:

> From then on, Pilate tried to set Jesus free, but the Jewish leaders kept shouting, "If you let this man go, you are no friend of Caesar. Anyone who claims to be a king opposes Caesar."
>
> When Pilate heard this, he brought Jesus out and sat down on the judge's seat at a place known as the Stone Pavement (which in Aramaic is Gabbatha). It was the day of Preparation for the Passover; it was about noon.
>
> "Here is your king," Pilate said to the Jews.
>
> But they shouted, "Take him away! Take him away! Crucify him!"
>
> "Shall I crucify your king?" Pilate asked.
>
> "We have no king but Caesar," the chief priests answered.
>
> Finally, Pilate handed him over to them to be crucified.

The Ideal King

Finding the right words to express the irony and shock of the leaders' response is challenging. Notice what is said and who says it. First, what do the leaders say? "We have no king except Caesar." The shock of these words is indescribable. How can Israel, the nation that was delivered from Egypt and specifically loved by the Lord, say such blasphemy? Did Rome deliver Israel from Egypt? Was it Caesar who provided for Israel in the wilderness? Was Rome the power by which their sin and guilt was removed? Did the people sacrifice their animals, pay their tithes, and make supplications to the emperor in Rome?

Israel's scriptural tradition was deluged with texts proclaiming the Lord's sovereignty over the cosmos, particularly his beloved people. Genesis begins with the King ordering his kingdom, making for himself a people, and defining their roles.[12] Yet, since those early chapters of Genesis, the Lord's people have rebelled against God's kingship in favor of any other power. The Lord's people rebelled against Moses[13] and Samuel.[14] When the monarchy was established, coups and rebellions were carried out against their own kings and even their vassal-kings. For example, Absalom rebelled against King David, and King Hoshea rebelled against Shalmaneser.[15] Each of the cases mentioned is where the Lord's design was set aside in preference for ease, personal gain, or political expediency. The higher, more challenging, and holy road the Lord calls his people to walk is rejected in favor of the downward slide to decadence.

Israel's leaders in Jesus's time are acting consistently. They, too, prefer the easy road of siding with the imperial power of Rome instead of walking with their true king on the difficult path of humility, love, and sacrifice. During the leaders' conversation with Pilate, they show their preference for political expediency by twisting Pilate's arm, saying they cannot let Jesus go because he

---

12. Gen 1–2.
13. Num 14.
14. 1 Sam 8.
15. 2 Sam 15–20; 2 Kgs 17.

The Ideal King

claimed to be a king, and "there's no king but Caesar."[16] Letting Jesus go would make Pilate an enemy of Caesar, the god of Rome and Israel's leaders.

The Old Testament juxtaposes two royal ideologies: the Lord's and those like the other nations. The two ideologies are compared in Deut 17:14–20. The confession of Israel's leaders in John 19 sounds eerily similar to the Israelites' demand for a king in 1 Sam 8. The king Israel's leaders confessed in John 19 was the epitome of a worldly empire built on raw military power, greed, and self-interested politics. Exod 19:3 says Israel was to be a "kingdom of priests" who, as Mic 6:8 envisions it, practiced justice, showed love, and walked humbly with God.

What Israel's leaders said was blasphemous. The leaders denied what the psalmist declares, "The Lord is King forever and ever."[17] What makes the idolatry worse is the leaders' identity. According to John's Gospel, the ones who said, "We have no king but Caesar" were "the chief priests." Israel's final authority on matters of theology, ritual holiness, and practice, those given the responsibility of leading the people in holiness, could have done better. The chief priests were familiar with Israel's history and Moses's prescription for the ideal king. Yet, when the ideal king is in their midst, they longed for a king like the other nations.

The difference between the ideal king, Jesus, and all his predecessors is rather striking. In 1 Sam 8, the Lord, through Samuel, warned the elders of Israel how their king would behave. The kings the people wanted, the kings like the other nations, would fall into the imperial state of maintenance through acquisition. In layman's terms, they would take the best of the people's things. First Samuel 8 included the word *take* many times in rapid succession, emphasizing the continual process the king would undertake. Samuel warned the people the king would take land, like Ahab. Or, like Saul, the best and bravest of society would be conscripted into the king's service, leaving every person to fend for themselves. Maybe like David, the king would seek revenge and kill his enemies or

---

16. John 19:12.
17. Ps 10:16.

even take women he found desirable, whether they were married or not. A marriage could quickly be annulled by killing the husband anyway. David did it. The point is how the kings were a burden to the people throughout Israel's united and divided kingdoms. Maintaining an imperial power like the nations comes at a price. Juxtaposed to those imperial attempts stands the spotless, humble picture of Christ.

Jesus said, "I have come that you may have life, and have it to the full."[18] Jesus's first recorded sermon in Luke's Gospel includes Jesus's own royal ideology, an ideology of giving.

> The Spirit of the Lord is on me,
>   because he has anointed me
>   to proclaim good news to the poor.
> He has sent me to proclaim freedom for the prisoners
>   and recovery of sight for the blind,
> to set the oppressed free,
>   to proclaim the year of the Lord's favor.[19]

Jesus gives good news, freedom, sight, and the Lord's favor. Jesus is the kind of king we deeply long for.

I Am a King

In all the Gospels, Jesus affirms that he is king during his interrogation by Pilate;[20] however, only the Fourth Gospel clarifies Jesus's kingship through Jesus's own words, giving fuller detail about the "king" of the Synoptics' "kingdom of God." The passage in view is John 18:36–37. About these verses, Meeks writes that this passage is the place where the function of the title *king* appears most clearly when the issue of kingship is addressed during Jesus's trial before Pilate.[21] If kingship is central to John's Gospel, and his message is principally about Jesus, then when it comes to Jesus's kingship,

---

18. John 10:10.
19. Luke 4:18–19.
20. Matt 27:11; Mark 15:2; Luke 23:3; John 18:37.
21. Meeks, *Prophet King*, 32.

The Ideal King

how does John understand Jesus's kingship? Thatcher argues John's Christology is inherently anti-imperial and often negative, meaning John "says a great deal more about what Jesus is *not* than about what Jesus actually *is*."[22] Thatcher argues that John's anti-imperial ideology and John's description of Jesus's kingship finds their most extraordinary understanding in the ideology of Deut 17:14–20. Those passages, too, are primarily negative in the description of the king.

John's Gospel is centrally concerned with the nature of Jesus's kingship. Jesus's kingship is established in John 1 through Nathanael's proclamation. Köstenberger writes,

> Jesus is acknowledged as the "king of Israel" at the outset of John's Gospel by Nathanael (1:49), though, as mentioned, Nathanael's understanding of the entailments of this term may have carried nationalistic overtones, which did not accurately characterize the true nature of Jesus' kingship. Misunderstanding is ever more evident in the people's effort to make Jesus their king subsequent to the feeding of the multitude in John 6 (see especially 6:14). While the references to Jesus as the "King of Israel" at the triumphal entry into Jerusalem in 12:13 and 15 appear to be more positive, the context there reveals that, once again, people do not truly understand the nature of Jesus' kingship.[23]

Nathanael may well serve as an example of the nationalistic hopes of the political, military messianic figure and how different Jesus was compared to those hopes. Modern American Christians often confuse the cause of Christ with political causes. Sadly, in American politics it is quite frequent that a candidate carries the name of Christ while at the same time espousing policies that are antithetical to all of Jesus's teachings. Like Jesus's first-century contemporaries, we fail to see how radical Jesus's life and kingdom really are.

The central Johannine passage concerning Jesus's kingship is John 18:34–38. Though Matthew, Mark, and Luke record aspects

---

22. Thatcher, *Greater than Caesar*, 7, 11.
23. Köstenberger, *Theology of John's Gospel and Letters*, 253.

The Ideal King

of Jesus's trial before Pilate, Jesus's description of his own kingship is totally unique to John.[24] This is another example of the Fourth Gospel's aim of presenting the nature and identity of the king, Jesus. John 18:36 "contains the only direct statements in the Fourth Gospel on the nature of Jesus's kingship."[25] What exactly do those statements say? The statements present his kingship in two ways, first negatively (what Jesus's kingship does not include), then positively (what Jesus's kingship does have). John 18:33–38 says,

> Pilate then went back inside the palace, summoned Jesus and asked him, "Are you the king of the Jews?"
>
> "Is that your own idea," Jesus asked, "or did others talk to you about me?"
>
> "Am I a Jew?" Pilate replied. "Your own people and chief priests handed you over to me. What is it you have done?"
>
> Jesus said, "My kingdom is not of this world. If it were, my servants would fight to prevent my arrest by the Jewish leaders. But now my kingdom is from another place."
>
> "You are a king, then!" said Pilate.
>
> Jesus answered, "You say that I am a king. In fact, the reason I was born and came into the world is to testify to the truth. Everyone on the side of the truth listens to me."
>
> "What is the truth?" retorted Pilate. With this he went out again to the Jews gathered there and said, "I find no basis for a charge against him.

Jesus's kingship does not include violence or power. If so, "my servants would fight to prevent my arrest." As we have seen, kingdoms of this world are built on violence. Violence and military power were central to Egypt, Assyria, Babylon, and Rome. Violence and military power were not central to Jesus. To have an effective military, you would need a large quantity of soldiers who are well trained and well equipped. Jesus's kingdom is not built on power, influence, wealth, or connections. What was Jesus's kingdom built on? Truth.

24. Meeks, *Prophet King*, 63.
25. Meeks, *Prophet King*, 67.

The Ideal King

In this carefully constructed passage, John alludes to Deut 17:14–20 by following the same pattern of discourse as in Deut 17:14–20. In Deut 17:16–17, three prohibitions are given concerning the function of the king: he must not acquire horses (war), wives (political influence), or wealth. Following the negative prescriptions in Deut 17:14–17, the text then describes positively the ideal king and his focus on "this law" (vv. 18–20). Not only would the ideal king focus on the truth, he was commanded to write for himself a copy of the law so he could have the law with him continuously.

Jesus is our ideal king. Jesus's power is not rooted in transient things such as military might, political savvy, or wealth. All these things can (and often do) vanish overnight. Jesus's kingdom is founded on truth, the rock that will withstand the storms of life.[26] Jesus's kingship also outlines the pattern of life his kingdom-dwellers must follow. Jesus's followers ought not pursue wealth, power, and strength. Yet, how often are we enamored by these fleeting things? To the extent we pursue these things, we demonstrate that our lives are like all the other nations. That's how Deut 17:14 describes what a king should not be: like all the other nations. Jesus was focused on the truth, and his followers must be focused on the truth as well. When our primary allegiance is to truth, we demonstrate we, like our King, are not of this world.[27]

Jesus's kingship is rooted in real power, truth, not mechanical power, such as an army or weapons. Jesus's rule over the cosmos comes not by force but by love and self-sacrifice. Can you imagine a more other-worldly kingdom? While worldly powers sustain their power through military might, the ideal king is not a military figure. As stated in Deuteronomy, God was the military leader of his people.[28] Jesus states as much in John 18:36. Jesus says, "My kingdom is not of this world. If it were, my servants would fight to prevent my arrest by the Jewish leaders. But now my kingdom

---

26. Matt 7.
27. John 18:36.
28. Deut 3:22, 20:4.

The Ideal King

is from another place." About John 18:36, New Testament scholar Leon Morris writes,

> To demonstrate his point [that his kingdom is not of this world], Jesus points out that his followers are not engaging in any military activity. Had he been interested in what this world calls a "kingdom," a necessary first step would have been to recruit soldiers. His servants would be fighting men. But now, as things are, it is plain to all that he looks for no kingdom from this world.[29]

Morris says the king expected by Jesus's contemporaries was a unique type of king. Warren Carter, in *John and Empire* goes so far as to say that the lack of armed resistance on Jesus's behalf is evidence that his kingdom is from a different world. Should the same be true for those who follow Jesus today? Should our lack of armed resistance show we are followers of Christ, trusting ourselves completely to the God of infinite wisdom? Jesus did not present a military threat to Rome. However, Jesus was threatening. Warren Carter writes,

> While Jesus' kingship does not present a military threat to Rome, it is nevertheless a real political threat to the way that Rome and Jerusalem order the world. His kingship participates in the completion of God's purposes, the establishment of God's reign/empire.[30]

Like the ideal king, his followers also pose a real threat to the way all the nations operate, though not a military threat. Christians' way of self-sacrifice, love, simplicity, and truth are diametrically opposed to self-promotion, greed, convenience, hoarding, and personal rights. This is what God desired all along.[31] The ideal king participated in expanding God's rule without the use of military power, influence, or wealth. Today, the true follower of Christ expands God's rule the way he intended through proclaiming and living the truth. In *The Prophet King*, Wayne Meeks writes,

---

29. Morris, *Gospel According to John*, 521.
30. Carter, *John and Empire*, 302.
31. Deut 17:14–20.

The Ideal King

> In 18.37, Jesus, having tacitly admitted to Pilate that he is king, explains his "kingship": "You say that I am a king. For this purpose, I have been born, and for this purpose, I have come into the world: to testify to the truth." Again there is mention of "coming into the world." More importantly, it is clear that the purpose of Jesus' kingship as defined here is essentially that of a prophet. What "King" is this whose "kingship" is "not of this world" (18.36), whose royal function consists of prophetic "testimony."[32]

Please do not miss what Meeks states. Jesus's description of his kingship "is essentially that of a prophet." Jesus does not describe his kingship in terms of military power. As a matter of fact, in Jesus's discussion with Pilate, he makes reference to the fact that if his kingdom were of this world, his servants would fight. Jesus does not deny he is a king, but rather not a king like the world. Jesus's power is far greater than the pseudo-power of military strength. His kingdom is based on "the truth."

Like Jesus, his emissaries were to embody the same mission as their king. The emissaries were not sent out to acquire power or wealth, but to pursue holiness and truth. The citizens of the true kingdom would demonstrate their true citizenship in the ideal kingdom by living according to the pattern of the ideal king. Just as the ways of Christ were hated by the powers at large, Christ's followers are hated in as much as their lives are lived as a testament to the truth that the ways of the world are ultimately impotent. The mission of Christ became the commission of his disciples.

Not Safe, but Good

IN C. S. LEWIS's *The Lion, the Witch, and the Wardrobe*, shortly after Peter, Susan, and Lucy arrived in Narnia—a foreign world existing within a wardrobe—they met Mr. and Mrs. Beaver and received a brief introduction to the world of Narnia. During this "who's who" of Narnia, Mr. Beaver told the children that though the White Witch was currently ruling Narnia, she was not the

---

32. Meeks, *Prophet King*, 1.

real authority of Narnia. The Witch was responsible for the dire conditions faced in Narnia, where it was always winter but never Christmas. The Beavers told the children the True King of the Wood was Aslan the Lion, Son of the Emperor Beyond the Sea. Upon hearing that Aslan was a lion, Lucy, the youngest of the crew, asked, "'Then, he isn't safe?' . . . 'Safe?' said Mr. Beaver; 'don't you hear anything Mrs. Beaver is telling you? Who said anything about safety? 'Course he isn't safe. But he's good. He's the King, I tell you.'"[1] Aslan is not safe, but he is good. Aslan, the Christ character in C. S. Lewis's *Chronicles of Narnia*, safely guides the various characters through their trials and ordeals; Aslan is not safe, though. Aslan does not remove the dangers. Aslan, like the ideal king, Jesus, never guarantees ease or safety for his image-bearers.

On the contrary, the King actually commissions his ambassadors with words of ensuing tribulation while ensuring ultimate success. Jesus told his followers that the world will hate those whom Jesus loves. Jesus told his disciples to expect such hatred because the world hated him first.[2] Jesus commissions his ambassadors, reminding them the mission is not kicks and giggles but crosses and crucifixions.[3] In short, there is nothing safe about following Jesus. Assuming such is foolish. But following Jesus is good.

Jesus promised a world reborn in light and goodness, and to prove his promise true, he himself rose from the darkness of death into the brilliant new life of resurrected glory. Those disciples who saw the glorified King turned the ancient world upside down. As ambassadors of the Ideal King, these disciples traveled all over the world proclaiming the risen King and his ever-expanding kingdom. The majority of the New Testament books are letters from the men whose experience of the Ideal King's new world so radically changed them they were called and compelled to tell this message abroad.

In the following pages, we will take a brief journey through the pages of the New Testament and watch the King's ambassadors

1. Lewis, *Lion, Witch, and Wardrobe*, 8.
2. John 15:18.
3. Matt 16:24.

embark on a mission initiated by the King. The ambassadors embody the message of a kingdom not of this world to a world in bondage to death and destruction.

Worthy to Suffer (Acts 5)

Not long after Jesus's resurrection and ascension, his disciples experienced the hatred that hung Jesus on the cross just months before. In Acts 4, the disciples were in trouble with the religious leaders regarding their unashamed proclamation of the Ideal King's resurrection in power and his coming kingdom. Two disciples, Peter and John, were seized by the religious elite for proclaiming the gospel of the Ideal King. After interrogation, the religious leaders gave them strict orders not to proclaim Jesus's kingdom message any further. The disciples, however, did not acquiesce to their request. In short, they said no (thanks, Captain Barbossa).[4]

The stern warnings of the religious council proved ineffective. The disciples kept proclaiming the King's message in word and deed, just as the King himself had done during his three years of active ministry. In Acts 5, crowds gathered from the areas surrounding Jerusalem that they might be healed by Peter and John. The power of the Ideal King surged through Peter and John, and the people were healed. The religious leaders were enraged and imprisoned the disciples. This time, however, they did more than warn them sternly. This time the apostles were flogged. This punishment is no slap on the wrist but a violent beating with various instruments. Peter and John, followers of Christ in word and deed, had a unique opportunity to test their own hearts as they underwent suffering for Christ. They passed. Acts 5:41 says, "The apostles left the Sanhedrin, rejoicing because they had been counted worthy of suffering disgrace for the Name."

The disciples celebrated what their Lord and King experienced. Their unwavering commitment to the truth, like Jesus's commitment to the truth before Pilate, caused them to suffer.

---

4. Verbinski, *Pirates of the Caribbean*.

Rather than cowering or being downhearted by such a brutal beating, they rejoiced in the honor. The beatings, bruises, and gashes in their skin were visible signs of their identification with Jesus. Jesus suffered for the truth; his disciples suffered for the truth. Jesus saw his suffering as for the greater good and ultimately from the hand of Providence; the disciples likewise saw their suffering for the greater good and from the infinitely loving pierced hands of Providence.

The disciples' experience with the Sanhedrin gives us an opportunity to evaluate our own commitment to Christ. Can you imagine a time when you suffered for the sake of the gospel and were joyous about it? Can you think of painful conversations you had to have about which you were grateful for the opportunity? If persecution, illness, and loss can be means of God's loving shaping of our own wayward souls, do we thank him for our infirmities? Or do we complain and moan about our misfortune? The disciples' experience is convicting.

Our King suffered. Rather than staying on his horse far behind the battle lines, Christ our King led the charge against the most tremendous forces of evil known to man: the world, the flesh, and the devil. Jesus's love for his enemies and his commitment to the truth cost him dearly. Not only did it take his life, but his death was one of excruciating pain. The writer of Hebrews tells us that because of the joy set before Jesus, the joy of reconciling the universe to himself and redeeming humanity, he endured and conquered the cross. He scorned its shame.[5]

Paul, from Power to Peace (Acts 9)

The conversion of the apostle Paul is one of the most dramatic conversions in Christian history. According to Acts 9, Paul was converted while journeying to persecute the church. The irony of this journey is remarkable.

---

5. Heb 12:2.

The Ideal King

Paul's way of doing business was firmly rooted in the ways of this world. Despite being profoundly religious and extremely well-versed in the Old Testament, Paul operated as an agent of religious persecution and violence. Unlike the ideal king prescribed in Deut 17:14–20, and later embodied perfectly in Christ, Paul believed maintaining power came through force. Acts 9:1 describes Paul as "still breathing out murderous threats against the Lord's disciples." Paul's anger and hostility toward the followers of Christ forced a visceral hatred for his own countrymen. Despite Paul's vast learning and familiarity with the story of his people, he believed the best way to stop the faith was to persecute it. Paul sought authority from the high priest to arrest (at least) those who followed Christ, whether women or men. Pre-conversion Paul is an excellent example of the blinding power of hatred and the foolishness that thinks force and violence can solve problems.

As a scholar of the Jewish people, Paul should have known that persecution will not cease true devotion to the truth. Egypt tried to destroy Israel, yet Israel's population boomed so much that Egypt had to increase the violence to address the problem. Egypt failed. When Israel and Judah were exiled to Assyria and Babylon, and the faith should have experienced extinction, those faithful to God remained despite the pressures. Daniel never gave in to the pressures of Babylonian kings. More near to the time of Paul in Israelite history, Rome's attempt to persecute the Jewish faith failed. Despite the long history of faithfulness in the midst of persecution, Paul set out to destroy the church. Like Egypt, Assyria, Babylon, and Rome before him, he failed.

While riding his donkey to Damascus, the Ideal King appeared. Paul, whether intentionally or unintentionally, responded adequately to the presence of royalty and "fell to the ground."[6] Jesus momentarily physically blinded Paul while at the same time spiritually opening Paul's eyes to see properly for the first time in his life. The same Paul who was filled with hatred for fellow man was so radically converted that he spent himself for his fellow man, working tirelessly for the sake of the gospel until the day he met

---

6. Acts 9:4.

The Ideal King

Christ again. At the end of his life, writing from prison, Paul could say, "I have fought the good fight, I have finished the race, I have kept the faith."[7]

Paul is an excellent example of the way of the world and the way of Christ. Before Christ, Paul was of the world. He saw violence and power as a means to attaining his goals.[8] Later, Paul saw only love as the means which will accomplish his purpose.[9] Paul's self-understanding before Christ was rooted in worldly status (education, birthright, religious affiliation); after his encounter with the Ideal King, Paul's former identity was rubbish compared with knowing Christ.[10]

In many ways, Paul's conversion to Christ is the typology for all conversions to Christ. While not every convert will previously be a persecutor of the church in such physical ways, Paul does represent well the state of the natural soul toward God. Before meeting Christ, we all are so aligned with the world and its system. Paul did not remain as such. When he met the Ideal King and swore allegiance to his kingdom, everything changed. Can the same be said for us?

Paul saw his former way of life as utterly worthless compared to knowing Christ. How do we see our former allegiances? Pre-conversion Paul found meaning in his place of origin, his vocation, his title, and his education; post-conversion Paul saw all those worldly identifiers as worthless. Do we have the same opinion? Do we still find value in our being born in the West? To what degree do we find meaning in our national citizenship, public vocation, or the letters and titles surrounding our name? To what extent have we "lost all things"[11] for Christ in actual behavior, not mere intellectual agreement?

Modern followers of Christ should honestly assess how much of themselves they see in Paul, not in the specifics like being a

---

7. 2 Tim 4:7.
8. Acts 9:1–2.
9. 1 Cor 13.
10. Phil 3:4–11.
11. Phil 3:8.

missionary, prisoner, and martyr, but in total life transformation. Paul is a clear example of what happens when a person encounters the Ideal King in his resurrected splendor and who confesses allegiance to his kingdom. Paul, who was once against Jesus, was converted and spent the remainder of his life with Jesus. As the King said, "Whoever is not with me is against me."[12] Paul demonstrates clearly there is no middle ground.

In Paul's letter to the Roman Christians living under the quintessential imperial power of Rome, Paul shows just how wide the gap is between those who follow Christ and those who follow the world. In a nutshell, Paul tells the Romans that there are two options: the way of power most familiar to Rome, or the way of Christ most clear in the path of the cross. Paul says in Rom 13:10, "Love does no harm to his neighbor. Therefore love is the fulfillment of the law."

Peter: Called to Suffer

Peter is another follower of Jesus who, with his own life and voice, proclaimed the royal proclamation he learned at the King's feet. Scripture attributes two epistles to Peter. Peter's First Epistle is centered on the theme of hope in the midst of suffering. His Second Epistle focuses on Christian knowledge. Both letters have something to tell us about the Ideal King and his already present yet fully coming kingdom.

Peter's First Letter contains some of the most unambiguous language regarding the identity of Christ's followers as inhabitants and participants of a different kingdom. Peter writes, "But you are a chosen people, a royal priesthood, a holy nation, God's special possession, that you may declare the praises of him who called you out of darkness into his wonderful light."[13] As a reminder, the "you" of this verse is identified in 1 Pet 1:1-2 as "God's elect, exiles scattered" abroad, those who have been chosen by God "to

---

12. Matt 12:30.
13. 1 Pet 2:9.

The Ideal King

be obedient to Jesus Christ." Peter inextricably links identity with Christ and obedience to Christ. Therefore, with Christ as King of this new kingdom, allegiance to him as King is not only affirming what Christ says but carrying out what Christ demands.

On the basis of God's choice, Peter's readers (including you and me today) are a "chosen people, a royal priesthood, a holy nation." These are not identifiers of any particular nation-state. No modern nation, Eastern or Western, could claim any of these titles. Only Christ's kingdom can be called such because only Christ's kingdom-dwellers seeks to live holy lives. The ideal kingdom aims to emulate its King, and the Ideal King is "holy, holy, holy."[14]

The holiness God expects from his people was prescribed in the Ten Commandments but later embodied and demonstrated through words and deeds by God-in-the-flesh, Jesus Christ. To follow the reigning King is to be different from the world, or as Deuteronomy puts it, not like the other nations. To claim allegiance to Christ while at the same time functioning as a member of this-worldly order is to commit treason. Identifying with Christ is not just assenting to his ideas but living his life.

But Christ's life was one of self-abandonment and suffering. Yes, it was. Peter anticipates such thought. The majority of his First Epistle addresses that theme. Christ suffered, and likewise, as Christ's followers, we will suffer. Peter actually says we were called to suffer "because Christ suffered for you, leaving you an example, that you should follow in his steps."[15] Peter follows this statement with concrete examples. "When they hurled their insults at him, he did not retaliate; when he suffered, he made no threats."[16] This statement includes expectations for Christ's followers. When we are insulted, we do not retaliate. When we suffer, we make no threats. This is not the way of the world, however. It is commonplace to return insult for insult, to threaten to "get even." Not so for those whose passport says "Kingdom of God." Behaving contrary

---

14. Isa 6:3.
15. 1 Pet 2:21.
16. 1 Pet 2:23.

to our King reveals our true allegiance, despite what we think we believe.

As best as you can, examine your behaviors, not your beliefs. We who claim to have been following Christ for a long time can probably think and speak the language of Christendom really well. But, the reality of our faith lies less in our words and thoughts but in our actions. Does the square footage of our homes, the make and model of our cars, the zeros (or lack thereof) in our bank accounts, hobbies, clothing, etc., look more like American values or the King's values? Honestly, I do not like my answers. Or, taking a cue from Peter, how do I respond when I suffer or when I am slandered? Do I follow the humble, meek path of Christ, or do I defend my honor and my rights? A tree is judged by its fruit.

What was the fruit of Peter's life? Peter died a martyr. Rather than leaving Jerusalem as the persecution's heat grew oppressive, Peter stayed. Peter, who once swore an oath that he did not know Jesus, swore an oath of allegiance to Christ that would have him nailed to a cross upside down. Peter's encounter with the Ideal King habituated Peter's entire worldview and created in his eyes that saw suffering not something to be avoided but something to embrace for the honor of the coming King.

1 John: God Is Love

During Jesus's final days in Jerusalem, before being unjustly condemned, Jesus gave instructions to his disciples concerning life after Jesus's death and resurrection. He demonstrated for his disciples in his words and deeds the now-present kingdom of God. By the time Jesus entered Jerusalem for his final Passover, Jesus calmed storms in nature while causing storms in the hearts of his witnesses. Jesus healed diseases, preached to multitudes, and even raised the dead. Jesus gave authority to his disciples to do similarly.[17] Despite all the power given to the disciples, Jesus reminded his disciples that the world will only know they are Jesus-followers by

17. Luke 10.

The Ideal King

love.[18] Love is the central element of the kingdom. This should be no wonder. God is love.

The disciple Jesus loved, traditionally understood to be John the apostle, wrote letters toward the end of his life. In his First Letter, John gives evidence of the impact Jesus's love made on him because love seems to be the theme of the letter. 1 John 4:7–10 says,

> Dear friends, let us love one another, for love comes from God. Everyone who loves has been born of God and knows God. Whoever does not love does not know God, because God is love. This is how God showed his love among us: He sent his one and only Son into the world that we might live through him. This is love: not that we loved God, but that he loved us and sent his Son as an atoning sacrifice for our sins.

God is love. The depth, mystery, and magnificence of those three words is without description. Love is a small word that carries enormous implications. Sadly, English has one word for love and uses it in a myriad of ways. "I love Taco Bell" and "I love my family" both share the same word but carry drastically different meanings (hopefully).

When John says "God is love," John is saying God is patient, kind, not envious, boastful, or proud. He is not rude, self-seeking, or easily angered. He keeps no account of wrongs. God takes no pleasure in evil but rejoices in the truth. He bears all things, believes all things, hopes all things, endures all things. God never fails.[19] God's love for humanity was demonstrated in sending his Son for the salvation of the world. God's Son, the Ideal King, came not to condemn the world for its egregious sins; rather, he came to pronounce God's forgiveness and grace through his own death and resurrection because of the world's heinous sins. Jesus, God's Son and our Ideal King is our ultimate example of what living as a member of God's kingdom looks like. Such a life is one of love, total self-giving for the sake of others, no matter the cost.

18. John 13:35.
19. See 1 Cor 13:4–8.

This self-giving love is what marks followers of the Ideal King. Jesus said by the way we love one another, the world will know we are his disciples. Yet, does it not appear that we in the church assume a different litmus test of following Christ? It appears that many in the Western church believe following Christ is evident by a particular set of theological dogmas that stand contrary to the philosophy of the world. Sure, following the Ideal King does involve a countercultural way of seeing all of reality. But that is not what Jesus said would mark his disciples. Others think affiliation with a particular stream of Christian tradition is what makes allegiance to Christ evident. Here again, Jesus's emphasis on the marking elements of true discipleship differs. The Ideal King says quite plainly how disciples of Christ live, act, and behave marks true discipleship. There is no way to get around it. If the King *really* rules our lives, our behavior will become increasingly like our King's.

The Great (Co) Mission and Modern Discipleship

Jesus commissioned his followers with clear instructions regarding his expectations. Examples from the New Testament showed the ways in which his ambassadors were obedient to the royal edict, no matter the outcome. The Ideal King sent his then-rather-small band of ambassadors to proclaim the arrival of the ideal kingdom through the life, work, death, and resurrection of Jesus, the Ideal King. Jesus sent his ambassadors not with vague instructions but with clear intent: go and do just as I have done. Love the world as I have loved you. From the apostolic age to today, the mission remains the same: to walk as Christ walked, seeking first God's kingdom and righteousness, bringing God's kingdom on earth as it is in heaven.

C. S. Lewis provides an excellent image of Jesus's expectations. In Lewis's *Mere Christianity*, he writes, "Enemy-occupied territory—that is what this world is. Christianity is the story of how the rightful king has landed, you might say landed in disguise,

The Ideal King

and is calling us to take part in a great campaign of sabotage."[20] The rightful, Ideal King landed and did so in disguise. Jesus looked nothing like the imperial kings that entered and exited the stage of history, whether imperial Egypt, Assyria, Babylon, or Rome. Jesus ruled without the massive armies, wealth, or political allies. Jesus's power did not ebb and flow according to the wishes of the people. Jesus established a worldwide kingdom without the need of massive armies, political alliances, or enormous wealth.

This King, whom the entire universe obeys, including death itself, was truly hidden from the world for the majority of his earthly rule. The powers operating just like the other nations tried ending Jesus's ascent to the throne by killing him. Jesus was placed in a tomb but did not remain there. After honoring the Sabbath, early on Sunday morning he rose from the dead, gathered his followers, and gave them the same mission he had fulfilled through the cross and resurrection.

Jesus calls his followers into the work of sabotage to carry their own cross. Jesus's followers were to engage in an activity: they would purposefully obstruct the way of the world by subverting it through other-worldly means. Jesus's followers would no longer abide by the destructive and delusional philosophies of the world. Ambassadors of the Ideal King engage in work just like their King by carrying their cross, clearly identifying themselves with the resurrected King.

Emulating Jesus is why we are here. In John 20:21, Jesus says, "As the Father has sent me, I am sending you." Jesus was sent with the mission from Isaiah: "The Spirit of the Lord is on me because he has anointed me to proclaim good news to the poor. He has sent me to proclaim freedom for the prisoners and recovery of sight for the blind, to set the oppressed free, to proclaim the year of the Lord's favor."[21] This was the job of the Ideal King. This is now the job of the Ideal King's subjects.

Before we rush too quickly into our mission for the world, let us count the cost. No matter what we say or do for the world, if

---

20. Lewis, *Mere Christianity*, 46.
21. Luke 4:18–19.

it is void of love, it will be worthless.[22] Jesus said the world would know we are his disciples by our love.[23] Love for God and love for neighbor will not only be the idea most prominent in his followers' minds; love will be the most prominent behavior of his followers. As Christ came to serve, his followers serve. Most succinctly, followers of Christ carry their cross in the same way Jesus carried his.

But the language of the cross may be used so frequently that modern followers do not grasp its meaning anymore. Jesus was crucified not for wanting to establish a spiritual path toward enlightenment. Jesus was charged with leading a rebellion against imperial forces. The placard above Christ on the cross accurately describes why Jesus was crucified: Jesus was the King of Israel, who would, through the cross, ascend to the throne of the whole world and establish his real, physical, universal kingdom.

John Howard Yoder's *The Politics of Jesus* has this to say about the "believer's cross":

> The believer's cross is no longer any and every kind of suffering, sickness, or tension, the bearing of which is demanded. The believer's cross is, like that of Jesus, the price of social non-conformity. It is not, like sickness or catastrophe, an inexplicable, unpredictable suffering; it is the end of a path freely chosen after counting the cost. It is not, like Luther's or Thomas Müntzer's or Zinzendorf's or Kierkegaard's cross or *Anfechtung*, an inward wrestling of the sensitive soul with self and sin; it is the social reality of representing in an unwilling world the Order to come.[24]

The cross, the central symbol of Jesus's ministry, of central importance to our bringing God's kingdom to the world, demands that we first seek God's cruciform kingdom in our own hearts. Benjamin Corey's book *Undiluted* seeks to address the radical nature of Jesus's life and ministry. In his book, Corey writes,

---

22. 1 Cor 13:2.
23. John 13:35.
24. Yoder, *Politics of Jesus*, 112–13.

The Ideal King

> For far too long, in much of American Christian culture, our movement has been defined not by Jesus—but by who we think our "common enemy" is. First, they told us the enemy was the people who wanted to teach evolution in our schools. Then they told us it was the people who wanted to stop teacher-led prayer in schools. Moving into the 1980s, we were told the enemy was the liberal agenda and the existence of legalized abortion. Most recently, Christian culture has tried to convince us that our new enemy is the "gay agenda" and the legalization of same-sex marriage.
>
> For too long, we've seen the gospel as something that exists to change whoever we define as the common enemy.
>
> For some reason, war is never the enemy. Cyclical poverty is never the enemy. A system that jails black men at shockingly disproportionate rates than whites is never the enemy. Corporate wealth and greed is never the enemy. Run-away defense spending is never the enemy. . . .
>
> And certainly, we are never the enemy.
>
> But what if we are?
>
> What if we are actually the most destructive enemy of all, and that we're sidetracking the Kingdom of God when we focus on fighting people instead of reforming ourselves? What if our own arrogance, greed, self-centeredness, and self-righteousness is actually the enemy who is harming the future of the Jesus movement the most?
>
> I think it is.
>
> I think we are.[25]

Could it be that Christians who acknowledge Jesus with their lips but disregard Jesus with their lifestyle is the biggest problem Christianity faces? G. K. Chesterton, in a letter to the editor of the *Daily News* in 1905, said, "The answer to the question, 'What is Wrong?' is, or should be, 'I am wrong.' Until a man can give that answer his idealism is only a hobby."[26] Chesterton and Corey point

---

25. Corey, *Undiluted*, 68.
26. Poss, "What's Wrong, Chesterton?," para. 7.

The Ideal King

to the importance of our life and doctrine, both affirming our allegiance to the kingdom, not merely our doctrine.

It appears churches are well equipped to instruct the intellectual framework of the Christian faith. Disciples of doctrine learn the Romans Road and other quick-reference texts for identifying personal sin and a personal need for a savior. Yet, those evangelistic tools rarely create lasting fruit. The message is not more important than the medium.

Near the middle of Jesus's Sermon on the Mount, Jesus tells his followers to "be perfect as your heavenly Father is perfect."[27] If Jesus was only speaking spiritually, then our outward physical behavior is completely meaningless provided we are spiritually united to him in faith. Jesus was speaking literally, though. Jesus had already been listing physical areas of fault, like lust and anger, by placing them under the penetrating light of his truth. He exposed the sins in order that they literally be corrected. What is the point?

How we behave before a watching world matters. Paul tells Timothy to "watch your life *and* doctrine closely"[28] (emphasis added). Life and doctrine matter; belief and behavior matter. When we have sin in our lives, we ought to think very carefully before casting stones. The only way disciples can truly begin working and amending their souls is through the work of the Holy Spirit. There is a verse from Galatians I have written on one of the walls in my house. The text is Gal 5:22–23 from the Living Bible: "But when the Spirit controls our lives, he will produce this kind of fruit in us: love, joy, peace, patience, kindness, goodness, faithfulness, gentleness, and self-control." The English here captures the reality of what Paul says: "*when* the Spirit controls [us]," which indicates that the fruit Paul goes on to list does not appear the day one confesses Christ, but after a process of learning to allow the Holy Spirit full control. Ambassadors of Christ will only represent the Ideal King's wishes if he lives by the Holy Spirit.

Through our Holy Spirit–empowered lives, our every word and action should herald the good news that the rightful King has

---

27. Matt 5:48.
28. 1 Tim 4:16.

come, the death blow has been dealt to the enemy, and all the ills of our present experience have their days numbered. It is precisely here that the mystery of following Christ comes to center stage. We would naturally prefer a list of actions to complete, words to say, places to live, and people to meet as a sort of holy checklist. That way, we would have certainty, and with certainty, there comes a sense of security. But Jesus would have none of that. His very life forces an endless number of blank checks, cleared schedules, and open plans. To ask what our King would do is to ask simultaneously the most dangerous and most thrilling question imaginable. Our consistently following Christ will undoubtedly take us into difficult, dark places. But, the darkness is greatest just before the break of day, when the sun bursts through and pushes back the darkness with renewed vigor.

Jesus's great commission to his disciples comes in Matt 28:18–20. Jesus says, "All authority in heaven and on earth has been given to me. Therefore go and make disciples of all nations, baptizing them in the name of the Father and of the Son and of the Holy Spirit, and teaching them to obey everything I have commanded you. And surely I am with you always, to the very end of the age." Jesus received all authority from the Lord God, the sovereign over the universe. Jesus, who was fully God and fully Man, humbled himself and became a servant to his creation. He washed his disciples' feet. He wept over death and despair. He touched societal outcasts and medical discards.

We are likely familiar with these details of Jesus's ministry, but we must remember *this is how Jesus understood and enacted his authority over everything*. He did not come and make a throne for himself in any imperial power. He did not seek security by having a better arsenal. He did not care about politically expedient friendships. Jesus was not concerned with the wealth the world could offer him. Jesus is King over this world precisely because he is not a king like others in the world. May His Spirit empower us to live like our King.

Amen.

Bibliography

Alexander, T. Desmond, and David W. Baker, eds. *Dictionary of the Old Testament: Pentateuch*. Downers Grove, IL: InterVarsity, 2003.
Alter, Robert. *The Art of Biblical Narrative*. New York: Basic, 1981.
———. *The David Story*. New York: Norton, 1999.
Arnold, Bill T., and Bryan E. Beyer. *Readings from the Ancient Near East*. Grand Rapids: Baker Academic, 2002.
Arnold, Bill T., and H. G. M. Williamson, eds. *Dictionary of the Old Testament: Historical Books*. Downers Grove, IL: InterVarsity, 2006.
Baumgartner, Walter, et al. *The Hebrew and Aramaic Lexicon of the Old Testament*. Translated and edited under the supervision of Mervyn E. J. Richardson. Vol. 1. Leiden: Brill, 2001.
Block, Daniel Isaac. "The Burden of Leadership: The Mosaic Paradigm of Kingship (Deut. 17:14–20)." *Bibliotheca Sacra* 162 (2005) 259–78.
Botterwek, G. Johannes, et al., eds. *Theological Dictionary of the Old Testament*. Translated by Douglas W. Stott. Vol. 8. Grand Rapids: Eerdmans, 1997.
Brotzman, Ellis R. *Old Testament Textual Criticism: A Practical Introduction*. Grand Rapids: Baker Academic, 2007.
Brown, Francis, et al. *A Hebrew and English Lexicon of the Old Testament with an Appendix Containing the Biblical Aramaic*. Translated by Edward Robinson. Oxford: Clarendon Press, 1907.
Carter, Warren. *John and Empire: Initial Explorations*. New York: T&T Clark, 2008.
Corey, Benjamin L. *Undiluted: Rediscovering the Radical Message of Jesus*. Shippensburg, PA: Destiny Image, 2014.
Craigie, Peter C. *The Book of Deuteronomy*. The New International Commentary on the Old Testament. Grand Rapids: Eerdmans, 1976.
Driver, S. R. *Notes on the Hebrew Text and the Topography of the Books of Samuel with an Introduction on Hebrew Palaeography and the Ancient Versions and Facsimiles of Inscriptions and Maps*. 2nd ed. Oxford: Clarendon Press, 1913.
The Editors of the Encyclopedia Britannica, et al. "Imperialism." Last updated Apr. 21, 2025. http://www.britannica.com/topic/imperialism.

BIBLIOGRAPHY

Fee, Gordon, and Douglas Stuart. *How to Read the Bible for All Its Worth.* 3rd ed. Grand Rapids: Zondervan, 2003.

Flood, Derek. *Disarming Scripture: Cherry-Picking Liberals, Violence-Loving Conservatives, and Why We All Need to Learn to Read the Bible Like Jesus Did.* San Francisco: Metanoia, 2014.

Fredriksen, Paula. *From Jesus to Christ: The Origins of the New Testament Images of Christ.* New Haven: Yale University Press, 1988.

Grudem, Wayne. *Systematic Theology: An Introduction to Biblical Doctrine.* Grand Rapids: Zondervan, 1994.

Harrison, R. K. *Introduction to the Old Testament.* Grand Rapids: Eerdmans, 1969.

Heschel, Abraham, *The Prophets.* New York: Harper, 2001.

Hill, Andrew E., and John H. Walton. *A Survey of the Old Testament.* 3rd ed. Grand Rapids: Zondervan, 2009.

Holladay, William, ed. *A Concise Hebrew and Aramaic Lexicon of the Old Testament.* Grand Rapids: Eerdmans, 1998.

Kaiser, Walter C. *A History of Israel.* Nashville: Broadman & Holman, 1998.

Kinnaman, David, and Gabe Lyons. *Good Faith: Being a Christian When Society Thinks You're Irrelevant and Extreme.* Grand Rapids: Baker, 2016.

Klein, Ralph W. *1 Samuel.* Word Biblical Commentary 10. Dallas: Word, 1983.

Kline, Meredith. *Treaty of the Great King: The Covenant Structure of Deuteronomy.* Eugene, OR: Wipf & Stock, 2012.

Köstenberger, Andreas J. *A Theology of John's Gospel and Letters.* Biblical Theology of the New Testament. Grand Rapids: Zondervan, 2009.

Kuhrt, Amélie. *The Ancient Near East: c. 3000–330 BC.* 2 vols. Routledge History of the Ancient World. New York: Routledge, 1995.

Lewis, C. S. *The Lion, the Witch, and the Wardrobe.* New York: HarperCollins, 2009.

———. *Mere Christianity.* San Francisco: Harper San Francisco, 2001.

Mazar, Amihai. *Archaeology of the Land of the Bible: 10,000–586 B.C.E.* Anchor Bible Reference Library. New York: Doubleday, 1992.

McCarter, P. Kyle, Jr. *1 Samuel.* Anchor Yale Bible 8. Garden City: Doubleday, 1980.

McConville, J. Gordon. *Law and Theology in Deuteronomy.* Journal for the Study of the Old Testament Supplement Series 33. Sheffield, UK: JSOT, 1984.

Meeks, Wayne. *The Prophet King: Moses Traditions and the Johannine Christology.* Supplements to Novum Testamentum 14. Leiden: Brill, 1967.

Morris, Leon. *The Gospel According to John.* New International Commentary on the New Testament. Grand Rapids: Eerdmans, 1995.

Niehaus, Jeffrey. "The Central Sanctuary: Where and When?" *Tyndale Bulletin* 43 (1992) 3–30.

———. *God at Sinai.* Grand Rapids: Zondervan, 1995.

Oswalt, John N. *The Book of Isaiah: Chapters 1–39.* New International Commentary on the Old Testament. Grand Rapids: Eerdmans, 1986.

Bibliography

Pew Research Center. "Religious Landscape Study." 2023-24. https://www.pewresearch.org/religious-landscape-study/.
Philo. *On the Life of Moses, I (De Vita Mosis, I)*. In *The Works of Philo: Complete and Unabridged*, translated by C. D. Yonge, 459-90. Updated ed. Peabody: Hendrickson, 1993.
Platt, David. *Radical: Taking Back Your Faith from the American Dream*. Colorado Springs: Multnomah, 2010.
Poss, Jordan M. "What's Wrong, Chesterton?" Feb. 28, 2019. https://www.jordanmposs.com/blog/2019/2/27/whats-wrong-chesterton.
Putnam, F. C. *A Cumulative Index to the Grammar and Syntax of Biblical Hebrew*. Winona Lake, IN: Eisenbrauns, 1996.
Richards, Lawrence O. *Expository Dictionary of Bible Words*. Grand Rapids: Regency Reference Library, 1985.
Römer, Thomas. "Deuteronomy in Search of Origins." In *Reconsidering Israel and Judah: Recent Studies on the Deuteronomistic History*, edited by Gary N. Knoppers and J. Gordon McConville, 112-38. Sources for Biblical and Theological Study 8. Winona Lake, IN: Eisenbrauns, 2000.
Ryken, Leland, et al., eds. *Dictionary of Biblical Imagery*. Downers Grove, IL: InterVarsity, 1998.
Satterthwaite, Philip E., and J. Gordon McConville. *Exploring the Old Testament: A Guide to the Historical Books*. Exploring the Bible: Old Testament 2. Downers Grove, IL: InterVarsity, 2007.
Smith, Gary V. *The Prophets as Preachers: An Introduction to the Hebrew Prophets*. Nashville: B&H, 1998.
Smith, Henry P. *A Critical and Exegetical Commentary on The Books of Samuel*. International Critical Commentary. Edinburgh: T&T Clark, 1904.
Soulen, Richard N., and R. Kendall Soulen, eds. *Handbook of Biblical Criticism*. 3rd ed. Louisville: Westminster John Knox, 2001.
Strong, James. *The Strongest Strong's Exhaustive Concordance of the Bible*. Revised by John R. Kohlenberger III and James A. Swanson. Grand Rapids: Zondervan, 2001.
Stuart, Douglas. *Old Testament Exegesis: A Handbook for Students and Pastors*. 4th ed. Louisville: Westminster John Knox, 2009.
Thatcher, Tom. *Greater than Caesar: Christology and Empire in the Fourth Gospel*. Minneapolis: Fortress, 2009.
Tigay, Jeffrey H. *Deuteronomy*. JPS Torah Commentary. Philadelphia: Jewish Publication Society, 2003.
Tsumura, David Toshio. *The First Book of Samuel*. New International Commentary on the Old Testament. Grand Rapids: Eerdmans, 2007.
Van Seters, John. *In Search of History: Historiography in the Ancient World and the Origins of Biblical History*. New Haven: Yale University Press, 1984.
Verbinski, Gore, dir. *Pirates of the Caribbean: The Curse of the Black Pearl*. Walt Disney Pictures and Jerry Bruckheimer Films, 2003.
Waltke, Bruce K., and M. O'Connor. *An Introduction to Biblical Hebrew Syntax*. Winona Lake, IN: Eisenbrauns, 1990.

BIBLIOGRAPHY

Walton, John H. *Ancient Near Eastern Thought and the Old Testament: Introducing the Conceptual World of the Hebrew Bible.* Grand Rapids: Baker Academic, 2006.

Walton, John H., and Andrew E. Hill. *Old Testament Today: A Journey from Original Meaning to Contemporary Significance.* Grand Rapids: Zondervan, 2004.

Weinfeld, Moshe. *Deuteronomy and the Deuteronomic School.* Oxford: Oxford University Press, 1972.

Wenham, Gordon J. *Exploring the Old Testament: A Guide to the Pentateuch.* Exploring the Bible: Old Testament 1. Downers Grove, IL: InterVarsity, 2003.

Williams, Ronald J. *Williams' Hebrew Syntax.* Revised by John C. Beckman. 3rd ed. Toronto: University of Toronto Press, 2007.

Wright, Christopher J. H. *Old Testament Ethics for the People of God.* Downers Grove, IL: InterVarsity, 2004.

Wright, N. T. *The Challenge of Jesus.* Downers Grove, IL: InterVarsity, 1999.

———. *Jesus and the Victory of God.* Minneapolis: Fortress, 1996.

———. *The New Testament and the People of God.* Christian Origins and the Question of God 1. London: SPCK, 1992.

Yoder, John Howard. *The Politics of Jesus.* Grand Rapids: Eerdmans, 1994.

www.ingramcontent.com/pod-product-compliance
Lightning Source LLC
Chambersburg PA
CBHW070454090426
42735CB00012B/2548